AN INQUIRY INTO THE GOOD

KITARŌ NISHIDA

An Inquiry into the Good

●

Translated
by Masao Abe and
Christopher Ives

Introduction by
Masao Abe

Yale University
Press
New Haven and
London

Frontispiece: Kitarō Nishida (1870–1945). This photograph was taken around the time he wrote *An Inquiry into the Good*. Photographer unknown.

The publication of this book was made possible through the generous support of THE JAPAN FOUNDATION.

Zen no kenkyū by Kitarō Nishida
Copyright © 1921, 1987 by Kikuhiko Nishida.
Originally published in Japanese by Iwanami Shoten, Publishers, Tokyo.
English-language edition copyright © 1990 by Yale University.

Designed by Richard Eckersley.
Set in Galliard type by Brevis Press.
Printed in the United States of America by BookCrafters, Inc., Chelsea, Michigan.

Library of Congress Cataloging-in-Publication Data
Nishida, Kitarō, 1870–1945.
[Zen no kenkyū. English]
An inquiry into the good / Kitarō Nishida ; translated by Masao Abe and Christopher Ives.
p.   cm.
Translation of: Zen no kenkyū.
ISBN 0-300-04094-6
I. Abe, Masao, 1915–   . II. Ives, Christopher, 1954–
III. Title.
B5244.N553Z4613   1990
181′.12—dc20   89-22657
                                                    CIP

10   9   8   7   6   5   4   3   2   1

Contents

•

MASAO ABE

Introduction

People in the West sometimes ask, "Is there philosophy in Japan?" This question is not surprising, for although Westerners have come to know a fair amount about Japanese art, literature, economics, and technology, their knowledge of the intellectual history of Japan is still sparse.

Yet this question has been raised even in Japan. Chōmin Nakae (1847–1901) once said, "Over the ages in our country, Japan, there has been no philosophy."[1] Nakae was a pioneer in the areas of democracy and materialism. After studying Chinese classics and Zen Buddhism, he went to

1. "Ichinen yū han" (One year and a half, 1901), in *Nakae Chōmin Shū* (The collected writings of Nakae Chōmin) (Tokyo: Chikuma Shobō, 1967), 168.

France in 1872 to study Western philosophy. Deeply moved by the thought of Jean-Jacques Rousseau, Nakae translated Rousseau's *Du Contrat social: Ou, principes du droit politique* and he later promoted a democratic movement in Japan. He advanced a materialistic theory without God, Buddha, or souls. To him, pure philosophy is a rational theory completely free from religious concerns.

The response of Japanese intellectuals to Nakae's statement has been mixed. In my view, one's answer to the question of philosophy in Japan depends on how one defines the term *philosophy*. If philosophy implies a purely rational and theoretical system based on logical thinking, as in the case of Descartes, Kant, and Hegel, then there has been no philosophy in Japan. But if philosophy indicates an existential, religiously oriented discipline as seen in Augustine, Schopenhauer, and Kierkegaard, then there has surely been philosophy in Japan. In Japanese intellectual history a parallel to these Western thinkers' "philosophical" works appears in the writings of Kūkai (774–855), Shinran (1173–1262), Dōgen (1200–1253), Itō Jinsai (1627–1705), and others.

The problem, however, is not so simple. In the West, philosophy and religion occupy two different arenas: while philosophy is a human enterprise involving the intellect and reason, religion is a matter of faith and practice in the light of revelation. In one sense, Western intellectual history is a process of opposition, conflict, and synthesis between philosophy and religion, reason and faith. Throughout the long history of philosophy, its practitioners have usually insisted upon its independence from religion and upon the autonomy of human reasons vis-à-vis divine revelation. As a result, purely theoretical philosophy, logic, and science are unique to the Western tradition. And even when the identity of knowledge and practice or metaphysics and ethics is advocated, rational thinking is predominant.

In India, China, and Japan, on the other hand, philosophy and religion are originally undifferentiated and inseparable. Truth in knowledge is none other than truth in practice and vice versa. But such an emphasis on the unity of knowledge and practice has resulted in a lack of logic and of purely theoretical doctrines regarding human beings and the world.

This basic difference between the Western and Eastern traditions finds expression in the reactions of Japanese thinkers to Western philosophy when it was first introduced to Japan in the 1860s following a three-century period of isolation from the rest of the world. Many Japanese thinkers steeped in Confucianism and Buddhism were attracted to the theoretical clarity and logical consistency of Western thought. The first Western philosophies introduced to Japan were nineteenth-century French positivism and English utilitarianism. Although these philosophies were not as profound as Buddhism and Confucianism, their practical character and rational and analytical way of thinking appealed to the Japanese. In the 1890s German philosophy took center stage, for Japanese thinkers discovered a profundity in German idealism similar to that of Buddhism. For a long time thereafter, German philosophy held sway in academic circles.

At this time, as Toratarō Shimomura states, "the Eastern spirit and national self-awareness as a reaction against Europeanization came to be emphasized, and thinkers directed their attention to problems under such slogans as 'the unity of Eastern and Western thought' and 'the rolling of all things into one.'"[2] Although their attitude toward Western philosophy was selective, it was not critical, and their efforts at synthesis resulted in eclecticism. To generate a truly creative synthesis, the Japanese had to engage in fundamental criticism of Western thought and radical reflection on Eastern thought.

An Inquiry into the Good (1911) is the first fruit of Kitarō Nishida's effort to respond to the need for this kind of synthesis. The attempt required him to confront cultural differences in thinking. The process of thought that underlies Western philosophy is demonstrative. Based on the principle of contradiction, it must be able to be discussed verbally and precisely. Western philosophy and science are its inevitable product.

Philosophical thought in such cultures as China and Japan does not necessarily require demonstrative arguments and precise verbal expression. Communication of thought is often indirect, suggestive, and symbolic rather than descriptive and precise. The thought process underlying this nondemonstrative approach does not simply rely on language but rather denies it; science, logic, and mathematics did not and could not have emerged from it. This does not mean that it is undeveloped and that it must evolve along Western lines. The Eastern way of thinking is qualitatively different from the Western with its emphasis on verbal and conceptual expression. This separation from language and rational

2. Toratarō Shimomura, "Nishida Kitarō and Some Aspects of His Philosophical Thought," in *A Study of Good,* trans. V. H. Viglielmo (Tokyo: Printing Bureau, Japanese Government, 1960), 193–194.

thought is typically found in Zen, which conveys its basic standpoint with the statement, "No reliance on words or letters; a special transmission apart from doctrinal teaching." The same attitude appears in Confucius, who proclaims, "Clever talk and pretentious manner are seldom found in the Good."[3] We encounter it in ink drawings that negate form and color, Noh theater with its negation of direct or external expression, and Japanese *waka* and *haiku* poetry. The Eastern approach must be sought in non-thinking beyond thinking and not-thinking. To generate a creative synthesis of Eastern and Western philosophy, one must include but go beyond the demonstrative thinking that is characteristic of the West and both arrive at unobjectifiable ultimate reality and give it a logical articulation by conceptually expressing the inexpressible.[4]

How, then, did Nishida strive to create an East-West philosophical synthesis? The following two quotations clearly show his basic intention and direction. The first comes from the preface of his book *From the Actor to the Seer* (1927).

> It goes without saying that there are many things to be esteemed and learned in the brilliant development of Western culture, which regards form [*eidos*] as being and formation as the good. However, at the basis of Asian culture, which has fostered our ancestors for over several thousand years, lies something that can be called seeing the form of the formless and hearing the sound of the soundless. Our minds are compelled to seek for this. I would like to give a philosophical foundation to this demand.[5]

The second quotation comes from *The Problem of Japanese Culture* (1940).

> Is there no logic besides the Western way of thinking? Should we think that if the Western way of thinking is the only one, the Eastern way of thinking is in an undeveloped state? In order to solve this problem we must try to consider it by going back to the origin and role of logic in our historical world. Even our thinking is fundamentally an historical operation—the self-formation of our

---

3. Arthur Waley, trans., *The Analects of Confucius* (New York: Vintage, n.d.), 84.

4. Toratarō Shimomura, "Nihon no tetsugaku" (Japanese philosophy), in *Tetsugaku shisō* (Philosophical thought), vol.24 of *Gendai Nihon shisō taikei* (A series on modern Japanese thought) (Tokyo: Chikuma Shobō, 1965), 24–25.

5. *Nishida Kitarō zenshū* (The Complete Works of Nishida Kitarō) [hereafter NKZ], vol.4 (Tokyo: Iwanami, 1978), 6.

historical life. I do not want to refrain from due acknowledgment of Western logic as a systematic development of a great logic. We should first study it as a world logic. Yet is Western logic beyond the particularity of the historical life, beyond being a mode of its self-formation? Formal, abstract logic may be the same wherever it occurs, but concrete logic as a form of concrete knowledge cannot be separated from the particularity of historical life. . . . Although we should learn from the universality of Western culture, which is persistently theoretical, the life that drives it at its foundation is not the same as ours. I think there is something quite valuable in our way of life. We must consider the issue logically by returning to the structure of the historical world and the formative function of the historical world.[6]

From these quotations we can extract the following three points as indicative of Nishida's basic philosophical attitude. First, Nishida valued Western philosophy and logic as universal and thereby recognized the importance of learning from them. And yet he insisted that even Western philosophy and logic are an instance of the self-formation of historical life and are not free from the particularity of the West. Second, though lacking in logic, the Eastern way of thinking is also a mode of the self-formation of historical life; Nishida wanted to give the Eastern mode a logical foundation. Third, Western and Eastern ways of thinking take different directions toward the self-formation of historical life. In order to create a truly universal logic, Nishida had to return to the origin and role of logic in our historical world and wrestle with the issue on that basis.

The first statement quoted above was written about sixteen years after *An Inquiry into the Good*; the second, written thirteen years after that, gives the basic intention of his philosophical efforts an even more explicit and articulate expression. Though his intention became increasingly explicit over time, it was already apparent in his maiden work, *An Inquiry into the Good*.

To clarify the significance of *An Inquiry into the Good* in the history of philosophy, I shall consider both the relation between Zen and philosophy in *An Inquiry into the Good* and the philosophical significance of the book in its contemporary situation vis-à-vis Western thought.

6. *NKZ*, vol.12 (1979), 287–288.

People often say that Nishida's *Inquiry into the Good* is based on his Zen experience. The actual situation is not this simple. While he was studying philosophy and writing *An Inquiry into the Good*, Nishida did pursue the serious practice of Zen. Consequently, his thought was surely influenced by Zen, and yet Zen is not explicitly discussed anywhere in the book. Instead, in his preface, Nishida states his basic intention as a writer: "I wanted to explain all things on the basis of pure experience as the sole reality." Of course, *An Inquiry into the Good* is a philosophical work that is intellectual, discursive, and systematic, whereas Zen experience is beyond intellectual analysis. They are entirely different. Accordingly, if we assume that Nishida's *Inquiry into the Good* is based on his Zen experience, then it is necessary to clarify the meaning of "is based on"—that is, the relationship between Zen and the book or Nishida's philosophy as a whole.

As Shizuteru Ueda points out, "It is inappropriate to regard Nishida's philosophy simply as a philosophy of Zen. At the same time, however, it is insufficient to take the philosophical uniqueness of Nishida's philosophy only as an issue in the rubric of philosophy without investigating its origins in Zen."[7] When Nishida asked what he considered the most fundamental philosophical question—"What is ultimate reality?"—Zen provided the direction in which he sought an answer. But for it to become a *philosophical* answer, he had to engage in philosophical thinking; he had to transform Zen experience into a philosophical answer.

This transformation has two aspects. First, the practice of philosophy requires a logical expression of Zen experience that breaks through Zen's trans-intellectual character. At the same time, Zen practice requires that philosophy be transformed by breaking through its intellectual rationality in order to awaken to the living ultimate reality. *An Inquiry into the Good* stands upon this mutual transformation of Zen and philosophy. As both a philosopher and a Zen Buddhist, Nishida transformed Zen into philosophy for the first time in the history of this religious tradition and, also for the first time, transformed Western philosophy into a Zen-oriented philosophy. In Nishida, then, the East-West encounter took a most remarkable form.[8]

An Inquiry into the Good has unique philosophical significance in relation to the state of Western thought at the time of its writing. The

7. Shizuteru Ueda, "Zen and Philosophy," *Risō* 514 (1976): 5.
8. Ibid., 12–24.

collapse of Hegel's absolute idealism in Western philosophy gave rise to division and opposition. One of the significant oppositions is that between the philosophy of realism, positivism, and empiricism, on the one hand, and *Lebens-Philosophie* (philosophy of life) and existential philosophy on the other. The former is represented by the dialectical materialism of Feuerbach, Marx, and Engels, the positivism of Comte, and the empiricism of J. S. Mill and Spencer. The basic stance common to these thinkers is a strict adherence to empirical facts and a rejection of any trans-empirical, a priori principles. This means denying both traditional idealism since Plato and two-realm theories of the phenomenal and noumenal. Closely related to natural science, this kind of philosophy is antimetaphysical and often atheistic. In contrast, the latter strand is represented by the *Lebens-Philosophie* of Schopenhauer, Nietzsche, Dilthey, and Bergson and the existentialism of Kierkegaard, Schestow, Unamuno, and others. These thinkers, opposing the former group's adherence to empirical facts and materialistic leanings, wrestle with the inner dimension of human existence, the creative development of subjectivity, and the irrational power of life. Although they usually reject idealistic metaphysics, they do concern themselves with metaphysical problems and religious issues.

Between these two opposing philosophical strands emerged a new branch of philosophy based on psychology, which as a discipline had been largely independent of philosophy until then. Keiji Nishitani points out that, as an empirical science divorced from philosophy and its categories and constructions, modern psychology grasped the phenomena of consciousness as directly given facts.[9] This trend toward a psychology based on the pure positivity common to natural science stimulated the emergence of a new philosophy represented by Wilhelm Wundt (1832–1920) and William James (1842–1910), as well as Gustav Theodor Fechner (1801–1887) and Ernst Mach (1838–1916). These thinkers advocated a new form of empiricism—as seen in Wundt's theory of "pure experience," James's "radical empiricism," and Mach's "empirico-criticism"—which emphasized pure experience rid of impure additions to so-called "experience." That is, they generated a philosophical standpoint by reducing experience to its pure and direct form. Behind the emergence of this kind

9. Keiji Nishitani, "Nishida tetsugaku: Tetsugakushi ni okeru sono ichi" (Nishida philosophy: Its position in the history of philosophy), in *Nishida Kitarō* (Tokyo: Chikuma Shobō, 1985), 109–112.

of philosophy loomed the historical situation of mistrust of both traditional metaphysics and two-world theories and dissatisfaction with positivism and materialistic philosophy. The only remaining possible basis for philosophy was experience that is direct to us. As Nishitani said, "What was demanded at that time was a type of philosophy that, while firmly based on direct and pure experience, could answer the fundamental questions dealt with before by metaphysics. It could not be a metaphysics in the traditional sense or a philosophy of scientific psychologism. Rather, it had to be a philosophy that could fulfill the demands represented by the two trends. At the same time it constituted a fundamental contradiction in philosophy. And yet a new form of philosophy that could overcome such a contradiction was needed."[10]

It was in this historical context of philosophy that Nishida wrote *An Inquiry into the Good*. "For many years," he states in his preface,

> I wanted to explain all things on the basis of pure experience as the sole reality. At first I read such thinkers as Ernst Mach, but this did not satisfy me. Over time, I came to realize that it is not that experience exists because there is an individual, but that an individual exists because there is experience. I thus arrived at the idea that experience is more fundamental than individual differences, and in this way I was able to avoid solipsism. Further, by regarding experience as active, I felt I could harmonize my thought with transcendental philosophy, starting with Fichte. Eventually, I wrote what became Part II of this book and, as I have said, certain sections are still incomplete.

From this statement we can distill three points: at this time, Nishida clearly regarded *pure experience* as the sole reality and wanted to develop his philosophy on this basis; he was not satisfied with the theories of pure experience expounded by the psychological philosophers; he wanted to connect his own theory of pure experience to transcendent philosophy or metaphysics by grasping experience as active.

Why was Nishida dissatisfied with Western philosophical expressions of pure experience? As indicated by the many references to Wundt and James in *An Inquiry into the Good,* Nishida was sympathetic to their ideas,

10. Ibid., 112.

but in his writings he criticizes them.[11] His criticism can be summarized as follows:

First, they explain pure experience on the basis of many uncritical assumptions, such as the claim that experience is individual and conforms to the categories of time, space, and causality. Such an assumption does not reflect pure experience in the strict sense, for it has already added a dogmatic idea to experience.

Second, they grasp pure experience not from within but from without, thus missing the true reality of pure experience. To see it from without means to analyze the concrete, dynamic whole of pure experience into abstract psychological elements like perception, feeling, and representation, and then to reconstruct them. In this explanation, living individual experience is generalized.

Third, true pure experience is direct experience, that is, experience direct to the subject. But in the above psychological philosophies, the observed consciousness and the observing consciousness stand dualistically opposed. Consequently, pure experience observed in this way is not direct experience. It is direct only in an indirect way. True directness is realized only from within the actual living reality of experience prior to the separation of subject and object. To grasp pure experience in its strict sense, we must return to the root-source of experience that is individual and yet trans-individual and universal. On this horizon of pure experience a new metaphysics is possible.

Through this critique, Nishida regrasped the "pure experience" of Wundt and James and shifted the basis of metaphysics from speculation to factuality. And from Zen he received the intuition that became the formative power in this new philosophical standpoint.[12]

The following quotation from the preface of *An Inquiry into the Good* provides an avenue to the consideration of pure experience in Nishida's sense: "It is not that experience exists because there is an individual, but that an individual exists because there is experience. I thus arrived at the idea that experience is more fundamental than individual differences, and in this way I was able to avoid solipsism." The ordinary understanding of experience is that first the self or the individual exists and then this self experiences something as an object.

11. For example, see "Ninshikiron ni okeru junronrika no shuchō ni tsuite" (On assertions by the pure logic school in epistemology), an essay written in 1911 immediately after the publication of *An Inquiry into the Good*, NKZ, vol.1 (1953), 210.

12. Keiji Nishitani, *Nishida tetsugaku*, 101–129.

Diagram 1
"Experience exists because there is an individual."

This perspective conceptualizes experience as if the experiencing self and the experienced thing, subject and object, are distinguished. This commonsense understanding is firmly rooted in the human mind. In the West this dualistic understanding of experience has been presupposed even in metaphysics. The metaphysical search for a universal truth or principle beyond the framework of individual consciousness has to transcend the realm of experience and to move in the direction of a trans-empirical, noumenal realm.

But in its real form experience is not such that first the self exists and then it experiences something as an object. Rather, the self is also experienced. In actual experience it is not that *the self experiences* something but that *the self as well is experienced*. This is why Nishida states that because there is experience there is an individual and argues that experience is more fundamental than the individual.

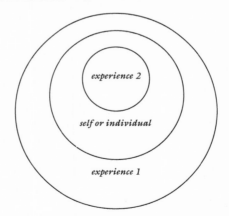

Diagram 2
"An individual exists because there is experience."

Experience in which not only things but also the self or the individual is experienced (Experience 1 in Diagram 2) is direct, whereas experience that is experienced by a presupposed self is indirect (Experience 2 in Diagram 2). A direct experience goes beyond the individual—it is fundamentally trans-individual. Direct experience is pure experience in Nishida's sense, and this is why he says the notion of pure experience enabled him to avoid solipsism.

As stated earlier, Western metaphysics transcended the empirical realm in order to find a universal principle and thus moved away from experience. But there is another way of transcending the realm of empirical, or ordinary, experience. This way involves not a transcendence *away* from us beyond the empirical realm, but a transcendence *toward* us, to this side, a return to a more direct realm of experience. It is a transcendence or, better, trans-descendence[13] toward direct or pure experience. It is upon the standpoint of this pure experience that we can establish a new metaphysics that is beyond the realm of experience in the ordinary sense and yet does not drift away from experience in the traditional search for a universal principle.

Pure experience in Nishida's sense has at least the following three characteristics.

1. Pure experience is realized prior to the distinction between subject and object. It is the common basis for subject and object because both the self and things are experienced equally in pure experience. In Nishida's understanding of pure experience—unlike in most forms of empiricism—the knower and the known are not two but one. Thus Nishida writes on the opening page of *An Inquiry into the Good*:

> To experience means to know facts just as they are, to know in accordance with facts by completely relinquishing one's own fabrications. What we usually refer to as experience is adulterated with some sort of thought, so by *pure* I am referring to experience just as it is without the least addition of deliberative discrimination. For example, the moment of seeing a color or hearing a sound is prior not only to the thought that the color or sound is the activity of an external object or that one is sensing it but also to the judgment of what the color or sound might be. In this regard, pure experience is identical with direct experience. When one directly

13. Yoshinori Takeuchi's terminology.

experiences one's own state of consciousness, there is not yet a subject or an object, and knowing and its object are completely unified. This is the most refined type of experience.

2. Pure experience is active and constructive. In ordinary empiricism, experience is understood to be passive and static, for experience is understood from the outside, indirectly. By contrast, experience that is grasped from within—directly—is active and creative. It is systematically self-developing and self-unfolding. It is a dynamic, unified reality that includes differentiation and development. As Nishida writes in chapter 1, "The directness and purity of pure experience derive not from the fact that the experience is simple, unanalyzable, or instantaneous, but from the strict unity of concrete consciousness," and, "Like any organic entity, a system of consciousness manifests its wholeness through the orderly, differentiated development of a certain unifying reality."

3. In pure experience, knowledge, feeling, and volition are undifferentiated. Ultimate reality is not merely known cognitively but also felt or realized emotionally and volitionally. The unity of intellectual knowledge and practical emotion-volition is the deepest demand of human beings, and it indicates the living ultimate reality. (And yet the will is the most fundamental *unifying* power of our consciousness and the most profound manifestation of ultimate reality.) In this regard, pure experience is a metaphysical organ in and through which one can contact ultimate reality (see first two paragraphs of chapter 5).

An Inquiry into the Good consists of four parts. After examining the characteristics of pure experience (part I), Nishida discusses the ultimate reality of the universe (part II), human personality and the good (part III), and religion, especially the problem of God (part IV). All of these problems are dealt with from the standpoint of pure experience; therefore, Nishida has developed the system of pure experience in *An Inquiry into the Good*.

In part II Nishida emphasizes that the problem of ultimate reality is not merely a theoretical issue but is closely related to the practical demands of morality and religion. Ultimate reality is realized in the deepest unity of philosophy and religion, knowledge and emotion-volition. To grasp true reality we must "discard all artificial assumptions, doubt whatever can be doubted, and proceed on the basis of direct and indubitable knowledge" (chapter 5). Direct knowledge that cannot be doubted is pure experience. From the perspective of pure experience, ultimate reality is neither phenomena of consciousness nor phenomena of matter but an independent, self-sufficient, pure activity. This is the unifying reality that operates behind all realities; the unifying power at the basis of our thinking and volition and the unifying power of the universe are fundamentally identical. This unity is not static but dynamic, and it develops opposition and contradiction from within, dynamically and endlessly maintaining ultimate unity. The universe is no more than "the sole activity of the sole reality" (chapter 10). Furthermore, our true self is not separate from the universe but rather is the very unifier of universal reality (chapter 11).

Nishida discusses the problem of ethics, especially human conduct, the freedom of the will, the good, and personality, in part III. The problem of morality, for Nishida, is always grasped in connection with the problems of truth or ultimate reality. The good is not merely the way of human beings but also the way of reality. The good is understood on the basis of reality. Accordingly, in opposition to the ordinary understanding of personality—an understanding based on the subjective self—*personality* is grasped as the infinite power of unity in terms of pure experience and is realized by "forgetting" the subjective self. "The true unity of consciousness is a pure and simple activity that comes forth naturally; it is the original state of independent, self-sufficient consciousness, with no distinction among knowledge, feeling, and volition, and no separation of subject and object. At this time our true personality expresses itself in its entirety" (chapter 24).

With this angle on personality, Nishida maintains that the purpose of the good is neither to obey the formal laws of morality as in Kant nor to seek for pleasure as in hedonism, but to fulfill one's deepest nature, to realize one's personality. This is why he bases his own ethics on energetism and his theory of self-realization (a realization of the life of the universe). To realize the fundamental identity of the self and the universe is to realize this infinite reality as infinite truth, good, and beauty: "We find that truly good conduct is neither to make objectivity follow subjectivity nor to make subjectivity follow objectivity. We reach the quintessence of good conduct only when subject and object merge, self and things forget each other, and all that exists is the activity of the sole reality of the universe" (chapter 25). Here we see the uniqueness of Nishida's understanding of the good and of ethics, an understanding deeply rooted in the Asian tradition.

In the beginning of part IV, "Religion," Nishida writes, "The religious demand is a demand that concerns the self as a whole, the life of the self.

True religion seeks the transformation of the self and the reformation of life. . . . and as long as one has even the slightest idea of believing in the finite self, one has yet to acquire a true religious spirit. . . . An absolute unity is gained only by discarding the subjective unity and merging with an objective unity" (chapter 28).

The religious demand is thus the deepest demand for the ultimate unity of the self and the universe. For Nishida, God is nothing but the basis of this ultimate unity: "God must be the foundation of the universe and our own foundation as well. To take refuge in God is to take refuge in that foundation. God must also be the goal of the myriad things in the universe and hence the goal of humans, too. In God, each person finds his or her own true goal" (chapter 29).

Nishida rejects both theism and pantheism and advances a type of panentheism: "Our God must be the internal unifying power of the universe, which orders heaven and earth and nurtures the myriad things in them" (chapter 29); "God is the unifier of the universe and the universe is an expression of God. . . . God is the greatest and final unifier of our consciousness; our consciousness is one part of God's consciousness and its unity comes from God's unity" (chapter 30).

God—as the basis of the unity of the universe—is discussed by Nishida not from the perspective of speculative metaphysics but as a fact of pure experience. And in pure experience this unity called God is experienced as personal, and as inspiring love and respect. God's self-development in itself is infinite love for us.

An Inquiry into the Good leaves a number of problems that must be solved in order to give a clearer philosophical expression to the standpoint of pure experience. One of the most serious problems is that of fact and meaning in pure experience. Nishida defines pure experience in chapter 1: "A truly pure experience has no meaning whatsoever; it is simply a present consciousness of facts just as they are."

Elsewhere, however, he writes that "pure experience is none other than thinking" (chapter 2), and that "the will is a fact of pure experience" and that true reality "is not simply an existence but something with meaning" (chapter 7). Pure experience is a fact without meaning, and yet at the same time it is full of meaning related to thinking, feeling, and willing. This apparent contradiction disappears when we understand that in pure experience prior to subject-object separation, act and meaning, or being and value, are not two but one.

Yet Nishida does not specify how fact and meaning are identical in pure experience and how the opposition between fact and meaning arises from pure experience. It is not clear how the separation between subject and object arises from intuitive pure experience and how it comes to be united into a systematic unity through differentiation and development. In *An Inquiry into the Good* Nishida's explanation of pure experience stresses the aspect of fact and being rather than the aspect of meaning and value.[14] This emphasis results in a tint of psychologism in the book, as Nishida himself recognized when he wrote in "Upon Resetting the Type" in 1936: "As I look at it now, the standpoint of this book is that of consciousness, and it might be thought of as a kind of psychologism. Yet even if people criticize it as being too psychological, there is little I can do now." But he continues, "I do think that what lay deep in my thought when I wrote it was not something that is merely psychological."

After *An Inquiry into the Good*, Nishida's task was to overcome this tint of psychologism and to clarify philosophically that "what lay deep in [his] thought . . . was not something that is merely psychological." Nishida had to stress meaning and value in pure experience and to develop a more logical inquiry into its structure. He had to reflect on intuition logically and to grasp the relation between intuition and reflection from the standpoint of basic unity.

Nishida attempted this task in his second major work, *Intuition and Reflection in Self-Consciousness,* which he called in his preface "a document of a desperate fight and struggle." In this book he developed the standpoint of *jikaku,*[15] "self-consciousness"—better translated as "self-awakening"—in which the inner relations between intuition and reflection, fact and meaning, being and value, are conceptually analyzed and logically grasped. He did this by confronting the philosophy then prevailing in the West—Neo-Kantian philosophy, especially that of Heinrich Rickert, and the philosophy of Henri Bergson. Through his effort to deepen philosophically the basic standpoint of his maiden work, Nishida moved

14. Masaaki Kōsaka, *Nishida Kitaro Sensei no shōgai to shisō* (The life and thought of Kitarō Nishida) (Kyoto: Kōbundo, 1947), 87.

15. *Jikaku,* one of the key terms in Nishida's philosophy, has no exact equivalent in Western languages. It is not a psychological or epistemological concept but rather an ontological and religious concept in which true reality awakens to itself and is awakened by us. In *jikaku* the subject and object of awakening are one. This is the reason we prefer the term "self-awakening" for *jikaku.* The term "self-consciousness" is usually psychological, and even when it is used in a philosophical context it refers to the modern intellectual and cognitive subject, which is only one aspect of *jikaku.*

from the standpoint of pure experience to that of self-consciousness or self-awakening.

At the end of *Intuition and Reflection in Self-Consciousness* Nishida expounds the notion of absolute free will, which is the culmination of self-consciousness. In this connection a confrontation with Johann Fichte was inevitable, for Nishida's notion of self-consciousness is neither psychological nor epistemological but essentially metaphysical.

Nishida in "Upon Resetting the Type" describes the development of his thought from the standpoint of pure experience to that of the absolute free will and beyond: "In *Intuition and Reflection in Self-Consciousness,* through the mediation of Fichte's *Tathandlung,* I developed the standpoint of pure experience into the standpoint of absolute will. Then, in the second half of *From the Actor to the Seer,* through the mediation of Greek philosophy I developed it again, this time into the idea of 'place.' In this way I began to lay a logical base for my ideas."

How did Nishida develop the standpoint of self-consciousness into the standpoint of *basho,* place?[16] With the notion of place Nishida moved from voluntarism to a sort of intuitionism. "Since *Intuition and Reflection in Self-Consciousness,*" he wrote in the preface to *From the Actor to the Seer,* "I have considered the intuition at the base of the will. I have had an idea, like Plotinus' idea, that to act is to see. For this reason I have regarded the absolute will as the ultimate."[17]

At this point Nishida realized the "seeing" at the base of acting, a "seeing without seer." Nishida did not halt his inquiry with this mystical intuition because he persistently strived to take a philosophical approach to the problem of ultimate reality. To be philosophical, he had to give mystical intuition a logical foundation. But he could not be satisfied with the epistemology of Neo-Kantian philosophy, James's theory of pure experience, or even the Bergsonian notion of pure duration (*durée pure*), for they were not completely free from the subjectivism common to modern Western thought. He approached ultimate reality by overcoming subjectivism through a confrontation with Greek philosophy, especially Aristotle's realism and his notion of *hypokeimenon.* By inverting Aristotle's

16. *Basho* is the most characteristic notion in Nishida's philosophy. It originates in the idea of *topos* in Plato's *Timaeus* and Aristotle's *De Anima.* In Nishida, however, "place" is entirely unobjectifiable and nonsubstantial Absolute Nothingness, which embraces and takes everything as its self-determination. See Masao Abe, "Nishida's Philosophy of 'Place,'" *International Philosophical Quarterly* 28, no.4 (Winter 1988): 355–371.

17. *NKZ,* vol.4, 3.

definition of the individual as "the subject that cannot become predicate," Nishida defined the most concrete universal as "the predicate that cannot become subject" and undertook to establish a logic of unobjectifiable reality. As I have written elsewhere:

> Nishida was convinced that for the individual as the grammatical subject—viewed by Aristotle as Substance—to be known, there must exist that which envelops it, the place in which it lies, and that this place in which the individual lies must be sought in the plane of "transcendent predicates," not in the direction of the logical subject. . . . What is referred to here as the direction of predicates is the direction of consciousness, and what is referred to as the plane of transcendent predicates subsuming the individual as grammatical subject is nothing other than "place" or nothingness as the so-called field of consciousness. In his grasping of the *plane of consciousness* as the *plane of predicates,* with Aristotle's hypokeimenon as medium Nishida gave a logical foundation to immediate and direct consciousness and seeing without a seer which otherwise could not escape subjectivism and mysticism. By so doing, he also laid a logical foundation for Reality.[18]

This logical foundation for ultimate reality is formulated in terms of the logic of place or the logic of absolute nothingness, which is not apart from the directness of life and yet is thoroughly metaphysical and logical. It is a logic of Oriental *nothingness* (*śūnyatā*) and it is essentially different from Western logic, which Nishida calls "objective logic."

After retiring in 1928 from Kyoto University, where he had served as professor of philosophy since 1913, Nishida began to write more and published many books, including *Ippansha no jikakuteki taikei* (The self-conscious system of the universal, 1930), *Mu no jikakuteki gentei* (The self-conscious determination of nothingness, 1932), *Tetsugaku no konpon-mondai* (The fundamental problems of philosophy, 2 vols., 1933–34), and *Tetsugaku ronbunshū* (A collection of philosophical essays, 7 vols. 1935–46). During these years he advanced such unique concepts as *action-intuition, continuity of discontinuity, historical body,* the *dialectical universal,* and *absolutely contradictory self-identity.* The most remarkable shift in his philosophical development was from the standpoint of place to the stand-

---

18. Masao Abe, "Nishida's Philosophy of 'Place,'" 370–371.

point of the world. Nishida's early work on the theory of pure experience had been largely concerned with individual consciousness in terms of ultimate reality; even when he had discussed the world and universe he had grasped them from the perspective of the individual. With *The Fundamental Problems of Philosophy,* Nishida shifted from seeing the world from the standpoint of the self in terms of individual consciousness to seeing the self from the standpoint of the world in terms of the self-determination of the world.

Most philosophers start with subject-object opposition and see the object from the subject—that is, they grasp the world from the standpoint of the self. From such a subjectivistic perspective the self is understood to stand, as it were, outside the world. But in reality the self exists in the world; the knowing and functioning of the self take place as historical events in the world. The world is not something that opposes the self but something that envelops it. And this actual and concrete world is the dialectical world, for within it our knowledge is the self-consciousness of the world and our expression is the self-expression of the world. In self-awakening (*jikaku*) the self and the world are dialectically identical in knowing and functioning. The self is a creative moment of the creative world. Logically, this actual, historical world is the world of absolutely contradictory self-identity, because the historical world is always moving from the created to the creating, from the one to the many and from the many to the one. It is this dialectical world or the world of historical reality that Nishida finally reached by deepening his theory of pure experience as true reality.

Nishida's persistent concern with taking a philosophical approach to the problem of ultimate reality is inseparably connected with a deep religious interest. We can see this in the preface to *An Inquiry into the Good*: "Part IV consists of my ideas about religion, which from my perspective constitutes the consummation of philosophy." In his last complete article, "The Logic of Place and the Religious World View"—the conclusive essay of his philosophical thought—Nishida argues that unlike morality, which is concerned with human conduct and value, religion is primarily concerned with the very existence of the self. When this existence is questioned, the religious demand arises in us. This question of our own existence is inescapable, for human existence itself is self-contradictory. It is in the realization of death that we encounter the deepest contradiction in our existence: we see God only through the realization of eternal death, because in the realization of our eternal death we realize the true individuality of our self in the face of the absolute; we thus find the ultimate ground of our existence in the absolute only through the realization of eternal death. This absolute is God, who includes absolute negation in Godself and descends to save even the most wicked. To die the death of the self is to see the absolute God and to be saved by the grace of God. Religion for Nishida can be properly understood by the logic of absolutely contradictory self-identity precisely because God is an absolutely contradictory self-identity.

Given Nishida's philosophical work after *An Inquiry into the Good*, we can argue that his entire philosophy is a development and deepening of his initial notion of pure experience.[19] *An Inquiry into the Good* provided not only the point of departure but also the foundation of his philosophy.

The theory of pure experience laid a foundation in a larger sense as well. Nishida's fifteen years of teaching at Kyoto University and his thirty years of writing exerted a great influence on Japanese intellectuals. This is not to say that his philosophy was free from criticism. During World War II right wing thinkers attacked him as antinationalistic for his appreciation of Western philosophy and logic. But after the war left wing thinkers criticized his philosophy as nationalistic because of his emphasis on the traditional notion of *nothingness*. Nishida was, however, neither antinationalistic nor nationalistic. He recognized a kind of universality in Western philosophy and logic but did not accept it as the only universality. Realizing the uniqueness of the Eastern way of thinking, Nishida took absolute nothingness as ultimate reality and tried to give it a logical foundation through his confrontation with Western philosophy. Forming his synthesis on the basis of historical life innate in human existence, which is neither Eastern nor Western, he neither established a new Eastern philosophy nor reconstructed Western philosophy but created a new world philosophy.

In this connection we cannot overlook a serious criticism of Nishida's philosophy by Hajime Tanabe (1885–1962), his successor at Kyoto University. Although Tanabe received Nishida's inheritance, taking the notion of absolute nothingness as the basis of his philosophy, he criticized Nishida's logic of place as being akin to Plotinus' emanation theory and

---

19. For a bibliography of primary and secondary sources in European languages, see "Nishida Kitarō Bibliography," compiled by Masao Abe and Lydia Brüll, *International Philosophical Quarterly*, vol.28, no.4 (1988), 373–381. For major translations and secondary sources in English, see the Select Bibliography.

as lacking a philosophical foundation for historical reality. Tanabe consequently emphasized moral practice and formulated a logic of absolute mediation.[20]

The next generation of philosophers, under the guidance of Kitarō Nishida and Hajime Tanabe, developed their teachers' philosophies in various philosophical arenas and came to be known as the Kyoto school of philosophy.[21] Although their philosophical efforts are diverse, all are positively or negatively influenced by the idea of absolute nothingness as realized in Nishida and Tanabe, and all attempt to create a world philosophy through the meeting of Eastern and Western thought.

20. Due to space limitations we cannot discuss Tanabe's philosophy and his criticism of Nishida in further detail. See the following translations and secondary sources on Tanabe: *Philosophy as Metanoetics*, trans. Y. Takeuchi with V. H. Viglielmo and J. Heisig (Los Angeles: University of California Press, 1986); "The Logic of the Species as Dialectics," trans. D. Dilworth and T. Sato, *Monumenta Nipponica* 24, no.3 (1969): 273–288; "Memento Mori," trans. V. H. Viglielmo, *Philosophical Studies of Japan* 1 (1959): 1–12; Y. Takeuchi, "Modern Japanese Philosophy," *Encyclopedia Britannica*, 14th ed., vol.12 (1970): 958–962; M. Inaba, "Zur Philosophie von Tanabe Hajime," *Orieus Extremus* 2 (1966): 180–190.

21. See T. P. Kasulis, "The Kyoto School and the West: Review and Evaluation," *The Eastern Buddhist* 15, no.2 (1982): 125–144.

A Note on the Translation

In this translation of *An Inquiry into the Good,* we tried to be as faithful as possible to the original text, avoiding paraphrasing and addition. We did not eliminate the apparent repetitions often found in the text, for we believe that it is important for the Western audience to experience the breadth of Nishida's thinking as directly as possible and to think with Nishida along the lines of his speculation. We tried to make the translation as readable as possible, of course, but we did this insofar as we did not run contrary to the above approach. Finally, to assist readers, we compiled the explanatory notes to the translation. Several people and institutions, both in the United States and Japan, were involved in the translation at various stages. A translation of part I was made by Thomas

Kasulis of Northland College and later revised by Christopher Ives. James Heisig, of the Nanzan Institute at Nanzan University in Nagoya, revised chapter I, offered suggestions, and provided a clean typescript midway through the translation process. Parts II, III, and IV were translated by Ives. Masao Abe went over the entire translation by checking it against the original text. The version that resulted was then polished by Ives for final checking by Abe. A Martin Nelson Award for Summer Research from the University of Puget Sound enabled Ives to work on the manuscript at the Nishida Archives at Kyoto University in the summer of 1988.

The manuscript also benefited from careful typing throughout the translation process. Sections of the first draft were typed by Earlyne Biering and Charlotte Tarr at the Claremont Graduate School. The second draft was typed at Haverford College and the Nanzan Institute. The final typescript was made by Janice Cable and Carol Avery with the assistance of two typing grants from the University of Puget Sound.

KITARŌ NISHIDA

Preface

I wrote this book during my years of teaching at the Fourth National High School in Kanazawa. At first I intended to develop my ideas in the section on reality and then publish what I had written. Hindered by illness and other circumstances, I failed to achieve this goal. In the following years, my thought changed somewhat and I began to sense the difficulty of doing what I had initially intended. At that point I decided to publish this book just as it was.

I wrote parts II and III first and then added parts I and IV. Part I clarifies the nature of pure experience, which is the foundation of my thought, but those who are reading the book for the first time should leave this section for later. I set forth my philosophical thought in part

xxix

II, the core section of the book. I wrote part III with the aim of expounding the good on the basis of the ideas presented in part II, but one can regard it as an independent ethic. Part IV consists of my ideas about religion, which from my perspective constitutes the consummation of philosophy. I wrote this part of the book while ill, so there are numerous rough passages; yet I managed to reach the end of what I had set out to discuss. I entitled the book "An Inquiry into the Good"[1] because I felt that even though philosophical inquiry constitutes the first half, the problem of human life is the central concern running throughout the book.

For many years I wanted to explain all things on the basis of pure experience as the sole reality. At first I read such thinkers as Ernst Mach,[2] but this did not satisfy me. Over time I came to realize that it is not that experience exists because there is an individual, but that an individual exists because there is experience. I thus arrived at the idea that experience is more fundamental than individual differences, and in this way I was able to avoid solipsism.[3] Further, by regarding experience as active, I felt I could harmonize my thought with transcendental philosophy[4] starting with Fichte. Eventually, I wrote what became part II of this book and, as I have said, certain sections are still incomplete.

Those who speculate might be ridiculed by Mephistopheles as being like animals who feed on withered grass while standing in a lush, green

---

1. We rendered the original title, *Zen no kenkyū*, as "An Inquiry into the Good" instead of using the common rendering, "A Study of the Good." For Nishida this book was no mere theoretical "study" of the good but, rather, as he himself states in the next few sentences of the Preface, a more practical, existential "inquiry" into the good as a major problem of human existence.

2. Ernst Mach (1836–1916) was an Austrian physicist and philosopher who was connected with the Vienna Circle of logical positivists. In his *Analysis of Sensations,* Mach argues that psychology and philosophy must be based on sensations. In moving toward a scientific and objective approach to mental phenomena, Mach took leave of earlier doctrines of the soul and systems of metaphysics. See R. S. Peters, ed., *Brett's History of Psychology* (London: George Allen & Unwin, 1953), 488–490.

3. Solipsism (Latin *solus,* alone, and *ipse,* self) is the theory that the self can know only its own experience, which does not necessarily reflect the way things are objectively (epistemological solipsism), or that the self is the only existent thing (metaphysical solipsism). Historians of philosophy often regard George Berkeley (1684–1753) and Johann Gottlieb Fichte (1762–1814) as advancing types of solipsism.

4. Nishida is referring to German idealism, which includes Fichte, Friedrich Wilhelm Joseph Schelling (1775–1854), and Georg Wilhelm Friedrich Hegel (1770–1831).

field.[5] One philosopher (Hegel) said he was condemned to think about philosophical truth. Indeed, for someone who has eaten of the forbidden fruit, such anguish is inescapable.

Kyoto January 1911

I first published this book more then ten years ago, several years after I wrote it. After moving to Kyoto, I was able to concentrate on reading and reflection, and this enabled me to refine and enrich my thought. I grew dissatisfied with this book and even considered taking it out of print. Later, however, various people asked me to reprint it. Feeling that I would need several years to set forth an updated, comprehensive statement of my thought, I decided to print this book once again.

I am deeply indebted to Professors Mutai and Sera,[6] who assumed the burden of correcting and editing the text for this edition.

January 1921

UPON RESETTING THE TYPE
With numerous reprintings of this book, certain letters came to lose their clarity, so the publisher has now reset the type. This book, in which I first organized my ideas to some extent, is my earliest published work and consists of ideas from my younger days. At this point I would like to revise various sections, but since one's thoughts have a living integrity at each point in time, I cannot change the book now, decades after I wrote it. I have no other choice than to leave it as it is.

As I look at it now, the standpoint of this book is that of consciousness, which might be thought of as a kind of psychologism. Yet even if people criticize it as being too psychological, there is little I can do now. I do think, however, that what lay deep in my thought when I wrote it

5. In Goethe's *Faust, Der Tragödie erster Teil*, Mephistopheles says to Faust: "A chap who speculates—let this be said— / Is very like a beast on moorland dry, / That by some evil spirit round and round is led, / While fair, green pastures round about him lie." Trans. George Madison Priest, "Faust, Parts One and Two," in *Goethe,* vol.47 of *Great Books of the Western World* (Chicago: Encyclopaedia Britannica, 1952), 43.

6. Risaku Mutai (1890–1974) and Hisao Sera (1888–1973) were early students of Nishida. Mutai developed Nishida's philosophy through the study of phenomenology under Edmund Husserl and eventually taught philosophy at Tokyo Bunri University. Sera became a professor of ethics at Otani University.

was not something that is merely psychological. In *Intuition and Reflection in Self-consciousness,*[7] through the mediation of Fichte's *Tathandlung,*[8] I developed the standpoint of pure experience into the standpoint of absolute will. Then, in the second half of *From the Actor to the Seer,*[9] through the mediation of Greek philosophy, I further developed it, this time into the idea of *place.*[10] In this way I began to lay a logical base for my ideas. I next concretized the idea of place as a *dialectical universal*[11]

7. *Intuition and Reflection in Self-Consciousness* (1917) is Nishida's second major work, in which (following his discussion of reality and the good from the standpoint of pure experience in *An Inquiry into the Good*) he tries to clarify, from the standpoint of self-consciousness, the relationship between intuition and reflection and the connection of being and value, fact and meaning. In his foreword to the 1987 English translation of the text, Joseph S. O'Leary writes that "it chronicles Nishida's eager search for a more sophisticated grounding of immediate experience in an account of self-consciousness loosely inspired by Fichte, as well as his long-drawn-out confrontation with the Neo-Kantian philosophers, Cohen, Natorp, Rickert, and Windelband, then at the zenith of their fame, but now, despite the reviving interest of a few historians, forgotten" (p.x).

8. In developing Kant's idealism with its view of the thing-in-itself and the cognitive subject as dualistic, Fichte emphasized *Tathandlung* (act) as the principle of the unity of cognition and reality, thinking and action. Specifically, in Fichte's *Wissenschaftslehre* (Science of knowledge), *Tathandlung* refers to the activity of the transcendental ego that posits or affirms itself, then limits itself by positing the non-ego, and finally posits the ego, the epistemological subject that stands in opposition to its object (the non-ego). In this dialectic, the act exists prior to subject-object dualism and constitutes the basis of consciousness.

9. *From the Actor to the Seer* (1927) represents a significant shift in the development of Nishida's thought. In this work he moves from his earlier voluntarism à la Fichte to an intuitionism, inspired by Plotinus. In *Intuition and Reflection in Self-Consciousness* Nishida had considered intuition the basis of will. Because his interest went beyond epistemology to a primary focus on the problem of ultimate reality, he rejected modern, subjectivistic idealism and moved to the intuition at the depths of self-consciousness, to "seeing without a seer," which he develops as the "place of absolute nothingness."

10. With his notions of place (*basho*) and logic of place, Nishida works out a logical basis for the intuition set forth in *From the Actor to the Seer.* His shift from voluntarism to an intuitionism involves a parallel shift from existential experience to logic—hence, to Nishida, place is not only metaphysical but also logical. As an expression for absolute nothingness, place envelops both Hegel's Idea and the concrete individual in all its irrationality, that is, Aristotle's substance as the "subject that cannot become predicate."

11. Nishida develops the notion of the dialectical universal in *The Fundamental Problems of Philosophy,* vol.II (1934), in which he states that the universal has three different dimensions: the judgmental universal (the realm of nature), the self-conscious universal (the realm of consciousness), and the intellectual universal (the realm of the intellect). The

and gave that standpoint a direct expression in terms of *action-intuition*.[12] That which I called in the present book the world of direct or pure experience I have now come to think of as the world of historical reality. The world of action-intuition—the world of poiesis—is none other than the world of pure experience.

Gustav Fechner said that one morning, while relaxing in a chair in the Rosenthal in Leipzig, he gazed in the bright sunlight at a spring meadow with fragrant flowers, singing birds, and flitting butterflies and became engrossed in what he called the perspective of the daytime, in which truth is things just as they are, as opposed to the colorless and soundless perspective of night found in the natural sciences.[13] I do not know what influenced me, but since long ago I have had the idea that true reality must be actuality just as it is and that the so-called material world is something conceptualized and abstracted out of it. I can still remember a time in high school when I walked along the streets of Kanazawa absorbed in this idea as if I were dreaming. In fact, my ideas of that time constitute the foundation of this book.

When I later wrote this book, I had no idea that it would be read for such a long time by so many people, or that I would live long enough to see numerous editions of it. I cannot help feeling like Saigyō:[14]

---

realm of the intellect is, in concrete terms, the realm of culture and the socio-historical world by which we enter into the dialectical universal through action.

12. Action-intuition (*kōiteki-chokkan*) appears in Nishida's later writings, including "The Logic of Topos and the Religious World-View." By this term he indicates that intuition is not a passive state but a formative activity as seen in great artists. We see, know, and work through the body in the world. Our self-formation is the self-formation of the world. In the body, seeing and working, or intuition and action, are identical through contradiction.

13. Gustav Theodor Fechner (1801–1887), a German philosopher and psychologist, expressed this idea in *Die Tagesansicht genenüber der Nachtansicht* (The daylight view as opposed to the night view). He attempted to integrate Hegel's *Naturphilosophie* into experimental psychology. In such works as *Elemente der Psychophysik*, he advanced "psychophysics," a theory of correspondence of mental and physical events. Erwin A. Esper, *A History of Psychology* (Philadelphia: W. B. Saunders, 1964), 235–236.

14. Saigyō (1118–1190), a Buddhist monk and renowned poet, was originally a court warrior with the secular name Satō Norikiyo. At the age of twenty-three he resigned from his court position and became an itinerant monk, travelling throughout Japan, composing poetry, and giving talks. His poems were compiled in the volume *Sankashū* around 1179; a supplement was compiled later.

I never thought
I would cross Mount Nakayama again;
yet, growing old,
I live long enough to do so tonight.

October 1936

PART I

Pure Experience

CHAPTER I

Pure Experience

To experience means to know facts just as they are, to know in accordance with facts by completely relinquishing one's own fabrications. What we usually refer to as experience is adulterated with some sort of thought, so by *pure* I am referring to the state of experience just as it is without the least addition of deliberative discrimination. The moment of seeing a color or hearing a sound, for example, is prior not only to the thought that the color or sound is the activity of an external object or that one is sensing it, but also to the judgment of what the color or sound might be. In this regard, pure experience is identical with direct experience. When one directly experiences one's own state of consciousness, there is not yet a subject or an object, and knowing and its object are completely unified. This is the most refined type of experience.

Usually, of course, the meaning of the term *experience* is not clearly fixed. Wilhelm Wundt refers to knowledge that is reasoned out discursively on the basis of experience as *mediate experience,* and he calls disciplines like physics and chemistry sciences of mediate experience.[1] Such kinds of knowledge, however, cannot be called experience in the proper sense of the term. Further, given the nature of consciousness, we cannot experience someone else's consciousness. And even with one's own consciousness, whether consciousness of some present occurrence or a recollection of the past, when one makes judgments about it, it ceases to be a pure experience. A truly pure experience has no meaning whatsoever; it is simply a present consciousness of facts just as they are.

What kinds of mental phenomena are pure experience in this sense? Surely no one would object to including sensations and perceptions. I believe, though, that all mental phenomena appear in the form of pure experience. In the phenomenon of memory, past consciousness does not arise in us directly, so we do not intuit the past; to feel something as past is a feeling in the present. An abstract concept is never something that transcends experience, for it is always a form of present consciousness. Just as a geometrician imagines a particular triangle and takes it to be representative of all triangles, the representation element of an abstract concept is no more than a type of feeling in the present.[2] And if we consider the so-called fringe of consciousness a fact of direct experience, then even consciousness of the various relations between experiential facts

1. Nishida's note is "Wundt, *Grundriss der Psychologie,* Einl. §I." In this chapter of the work, translated by Charles Hubbard Judd, Wilhelm Wundt (1832–1920), a German philosopher and psychologist, writes that "the standpoint of natural science may . . . be designated as that of *mediate experience,* since it is possible only after abstracting from the subjective factor present in all actual experience; the standpoint of psychology, on the other hand, may be designated as that of *immediate experience,* since it purposely does away with the abstraction and all its consequences." Wilhelm Wundt, *Outlines of Psychology* (Leipzig: Wilhelm Engelmann, 1897), 3. Wundt wrote prolifically on such topics as philosophy, psychology, physiology, ethics, and logic and established the first laboratory for experimental psychology. Advancing a type of voluntarism, he opposed the sensationalism of thinkers like Mach.

2. Nishida's note is "James, *The Principles of Psychology,* vol.I, chap.VII." Nishida's personal library, now mainly in an archive at Kyoto University, includes the 1890 edition published in New York by Henry Holt.

is—like sensation and perception—a kind of pure experience.[3] Granting this, what is the state of the phenomena of feeling and will? Obviously, feelings of pleasure and displeasure are present consciousness; and the will, though oriented toward a goal in the future, is always felt as desire in the present.

Let us now consider briefly the characteristics of this direct, pure experience that is the cause of all mental phenomena. The first issue is whether pure experience is simple or complex. Given that direct, pure experience is constructed out of past experience and can be analyzed later into its single elements, we can consider it complex. Yet no matter how complex it might be, at the moment it occurs, pure experience is always a simple fact. When a reappearing past consciousness has been unified within present consciousness as a single element and has obtained a new meaning, it is of course no longer identical with the original past consciousness.[4] Similarly, when we analyze a present consciousness, what we are left with after analysis is no longer identical with that present consciousness. From the perspective of pure experience, then, all experiences are distinct and in each case they are simple and original.

Next, we need to determine the extent of the synthesis of pure experience. The present of pure experience is not the present in thought, for once one thinks about the present, it is no longer present. In the present as a fact of consciousness there must be some temporal duration.[5] The focus of consciousness is at all times the present, and the sphere of

---

3. Nishida's note is "James, A World of Pure Experience." James writes in this essay (originally published in 1904 in the *Journal of Philosophy, Psychology, and Scientific Methods*) that "the relations that connect experiences must themselves be experienced relations, and any kind of relation experienced must be accounted as 'real' as anything else in the system." John J. McDermott, ed., *The Writings of William James* (Chicago: University of Chicago Press, 1977), 195.

4. Nishida's note reads "Stout, *Analytical Psychology*, vol.II, p.45." In this section of *Analytical Psychology* (New York: Swan Sonnenschein, 1902), George Frederick Stout writes, "the only particular which is actually operative is the given particular. It is the special piece of sugar as seen by me at this special moment which recalls the sweet taste. The past particular experiences of other particular bits of sugar no longer exist, and therefore cannot operate." Stout (1860–1944) was an English philosopher and psychologist.

5. Nishida's note is "James, *The Principles of Psychology*, vol.I, chap.XV." In this chapter, "The Perception of Time," James writes, "In short, the practically cognized present is no knife-edge but a saddle-back, with a certain breadth of its own on which we sit perched, and from which we look in two directions into time." William James, *The Principles of Psychology*, vol.I (New York: Henry Holt, 1890), 609.

pure experience coincides with the sphere of attention. But the sphere of pure experience is not necessarily limited to a single focus of attention. Without adding the least bit of thought, we can shift our attention within the state where subject and object have not yet separated. For example, a climber's determined ascent of a cliff and a musician's performance of a piece that has been mastered through practice are examples of what G. F. Stout calls a "perceptual train."[6] Such a mental state may accompany the instinctual behavior of animals as well.

In these mental phenomena, perception maintains a strict unity and connectedness; when consciousness moves from one thing to the next, attention is always directed toward the things perceived and each act gives rise to the next without the slightest crack between them for thinking to enter. Compared with an instantaneous perception, a perceptual train allows for shifts of attention and temporal duration, but in terms of directness and the union of subject and object, there is no difference. Because a so-called instantaneous perception is actually a consolidated construct of a complex experience, the two types of perception differ merely in degree, not in kind. Thus, pure experience is not necessarily limited to simple sensations. In the strict sense of the expression as used by psychologists, a simple sensation is actually a hypothetical entity resulting from scholarly analysis, not a direct, concrete experience.

The directness and purity of pure experience derive not from the experience's being simple, unanalyzable, or instantaneous, but from the strict unity of concrete consciousness. Consciousness does not arise from the consolidation of what psychologists call simple mental elements; it constitutes a single system from the start. The consciousness of a newborn infant is most likely a chaotic unity in which even the distinction between light and darkness is unclear. From this condition myriad states of consciousness develop through differentiation. Even so, no matter how finely differentiated these states may be, at no time do we lose the fundamentally systematic form of consciousness. Concrete consciousness

6. Nishida's note is "Stout, *Manual of Psychology*, p.252." Stout does not use the expression "perceptual train" on the page noted by Nishida, but he discusses the persistence demonstrated by squirrels in opening hickory nuts: "Just because the impulse is a tendency towards an end, it guides the course of the action. When the action enters into a phase which checks instead of furthering the return to equilibrium, the current of activity diverts itself into a relatively new channel. This process would not be a process towards an end, if it could persist without variation in an unsuccessful course." George Frederick Stout, *A Manual of Psychology* (New York: Hinds & Noble, 1899), 252–253.

that is direct to us always appears in this form. Not even an instantaneous perception diverges from this. For example, when we think we have perceived at a glance the entirety of a thing, careful investigation will reveal that attention shifted automatically through eye movement, enabling us to know the whole. Such systematic development is the original form of consciousness, and as long as the unity maintains itself and consciousness develops of its own accord, we do not lose our foothold in pure experience.

This holds true for representational and perceptual experiences as well. When a system of representations develops by itself, the event as a whole is a pure experience. An example of this is Goethe's intuitive composition of a poem while dreaming. In perceptual experiences, attention is directed by external objects, so such experience might seem to lack a unity of consciousness. But behind the perceptual activity an unconscious unifying power must be functioning, and it is this that guides attention. In contrast, a representational experience, however unified it might be, is necessarily a subjective action and seems to diverge from experience of the pure sort. When its unity occurs by itself and it coalesces on its own, though, we must recognize even a representational experience as a pure experience. For example, when its unity is not interrupted by external factors, a dream is readily confused with a perceptual experience. There is no fundamental distinction between internal and external in experience, and what makes an experience pure is its unity, not its kind. When strictly combined with a sensation, even a representation is a single experience. But when a representation is detached from the unity realized in the present and related to some other consciousness it is no longer a present experience, for it has become meaning. Moreover, when it stands alone, a representation is—like a dream—readily confused with a perception. And the reason a sensation is always considered an experience is that it invariably constitutes the focus of attention and the center of unity.

Let us now delineate in more detail the significance of the unity of consciousness and the character of pure experience. Like any organic entity, a system of consciousness manifests its wholeness through the orderly, differentiated development of a certain unifying reality.[7] When

---

7. "A certain unifying reality" is a rendering of the term *tōitsuteki arumono*, literally, "a unifying certain thing." Throughout this translation, *arumono* is rendered "a certain reality" rather than "a certain thing" or "a certain entity" in order to avoid the limited, substantialist nuance of "thing" or "entity." In several sentences that include the term reality (as in ultimate reality) we render this expression "a certain unifying factor" in order to avoid confusion.

a consciousness starts to emerge, a unifying activity—in the form of a feeling of inclination—accompanies it. This activity directs our attention, and it is unconscious when the unity is strict or undisturbed from without; otherwise it appears in consciousness as representations and diverges immediately from the state of pure experience. That is, as long as the unifying activity is functioning, the whole is actuality—it is pure experience.

Assuming that we can argue that consciousness is entirely impulsive, and that as voluntarists maintain the will is the fundamental form of consciousness, then the mode of the development of consciousness is, in a broad sense, the mode of the development of the will, and the aforementioned unifying inclination is the goal of the will. Pure experience is an animated state with maximum freedom in which there is no gap between the demands of the will and their fulfillment. Of course, relative to a selective will, control by an impulsive will might be seen as a restriction of the will. In a selective will, freedom has already been lost; yet when we then train the will, it again becomes impulsive. The essence of the will lies not in desire concerning the future but in present activity. Physical actions accompanying the will are not necessary elements of it. From a purely psychological viewpoint, the will is an internal, apperceptive activity of consciousness, and apart from this unifying activity there is no distinctive phenomenon called the will. In fact, the zenith of this unifying activity is the will. Like the will, thinking is a kind of apperceptive activity, but its unity is simply subjective whereas the will involves a unity of the subject and object. For this reason the will always functions in the present.[8]

I have claimed that pure experience is the intuition of facts just as they are and that it is devoid of meaning. When expressed in this way, pure experience might be considered a nebulous, nondiscriminating condition. However, because various meanings and judgments derive from distinctions in the experience itself, these distinctions are not imparted by the meanings or judgments: experience always includes an aspect of discrimination. For example, one looks at a color and judges it to be blue, but this judgment does not make the original color sensation any clearer; the judgment has simply established a relationship between the

8. Nishida's note is "Schopenhauer, *Die Welt als Wille und Vorstellung*, §54." In *The World as Will and Representation*, Arthur Schopenhauer (1788–1860) sets forth a notion of a universal will that expresses itself as the world and all that it contains.

present sensation and similar sensations in the past. Or if I take a single visual experience to be of a desk and make various judgments about it, no richness is added to the content of the experience itself. The meanings of, or judgments about, an experience are simply expressions of its relation to other experiences; they do not enrich the content of the experience. Meanings or judgments are an abstracted part of the original experience, and compared with the original experience they are meager in content. There are of course times when, in recollecting the original experience, we become conscious of something that was unconscious, but this is nothing more than our attending to a part of the original experience that was not previously an object of attention. Meaning or judgment thus does not add anything new to the experience.

Assuming that pure experience is endowed with discriminations, what are the meanings or judgments added to it and how do they relate to pure experience? People usually argue that when pure experience is connected to objective reality it generates meaning and takes the form of judgments, but from the perspective of my theory of pure experience, we cannot leave the sphere of pure experience. Meanings or judgments derive from the connection of a present consciousness to past consciousnesses; meanings and judgments are based on the unifying activity in the great network of consciousness. They indicate the relation between present consciousness and other consciousnesses, and therefore merely express the position of present consciousness within the network of consciousness. For example, when one interprets an auditory sensation to be the sound of a bell, one has merely established the sensation's position relative to past experiences.

Regardless of its nature, as long as consciousness maintains a strict unity it is a pure experience: it is simply a fact. But when the unity is broken and a present consciousness enters into a relation with other consciousnesses it generates meanings and judgments. In contrast to pure experiences that reveal themselves to us directly, the consciousness of the past has now become activated and connects with one part of present consciousness while conflicting with another. The state of pure experience thus breaks apart and crumbles away. Such things as meanings and judgments are states of this disunity. Upon careful reflection, however, we see that even these unities and disunities differ only in degree; there is neither completely unified consciousness nor completely disunified consciousness. All consciousness develops systematically. Just as an instantaneous knowing implies various oppositions and shifts, so behind

9

the relational consciousness that is seen in meanings and judgments must there be a unifying consciousness which makes the relations possible. As Wundt says, all judgments derive from the analysis of complex representations.[9]

When a judgment has been gradually refined and its unity has become strict, the judgment assumes the form of a pure experience. For example, as one matures in an art, that which at first was conscious becomes unconscious. Taking this a step farther, we are led to the conclusion that pure experience and the meanings or judgments it generates manifest the two sides of consciousness: they are different facets of one and the same thing. In a certain respect, consciousness possesses unity; but at the same time there must be an aspect of development through differentiation. And as William James explains in his essay "The Stream of Thought," consciousness is not stuck in its present, for it implicitly relates to other consciousnesses. The present can always be seen as part of a great system, and development through differentiation is the activity of a still greater unity.

If we thus regard even meaning as derived from the activity of a great unity, then does pure experience transcend its own sphere? When it relates to the past through memory and to the future through the will, does pure experience transcend the present? Psychologists hold that consciousness is an event, not a thing, and that it is therefore new at each moment and never repeated. I believe that their perspective diverges from the theory of pure experience. Do not psychologists reason from the character of time, in which the past does not recur and the future has not yet arrived? From the standpoint of pure experience, must we not consider consciousnesses with identical content as being identical? For example, in thinking or willing, when a representation of a goal is continuously functioning, we must consider it a single entity; likewise, even when a unifying activity is interrupted in its functioning through time, we must still consider it a single entity.

9. Nishida's note is "Wundt, *Logik,* Bd.i, Abs.iii, Kap.i." Nishida's personal library at Kyoto University includes the work, which has the full title of *Logik: Eine Untersuchung der Prinzipien der Erkenntnis und der Methoden wissenschaftlicher Forschung.* The first volume is entitled *Allgemeine Logik und Erkenntnistheorie.*

CHAPTER 2

Thinking

In psychological terms, thinking is the activity that determines relations between representations and unifies them. Its simplest form is judgment, which connects two representations by determining a relation between them. But in making a judgment we are not connecting two independent representations—we are actually analyzing a single representation in its entirety. For example, the judgment "The horse runs" derives from analysis of a single representation: "the running horse." Facts of pure experience always underlie judgments, and for this reason we can connect the subject and object representations in a judgment.

It is not always the case that first an entire representation appears and then analysis begins. Sometimes a representation of a grammatical subject emerges, which triggers a series of associations that continue until we choose one. Even in this case, however, the entire representation containing the individual subject and object representations must come forth in order for us to decide on a certain association. Although the representation was operating implicitly from the start, we can make a judgment only when it becomes manifest.

The idea that pure experience must exist at the base of judgments pertains not only to judgments of facts but also to purely rational judgments. Even the axioms of geometry are based on a kind of intuition. No matter how abstract two concepts might be, the experience of a unifying reality underlies the comparison and judgment of them. This accounts for what is called necessity in thinking. And as noted earlier, if not only perceptions but also the consciousness of relations is "experience," then we can argue that a fact of pure experience underlies a purely rational judgment as well. This holds even for judgments that result from inference; just as Locke argues that there must be an intuitional verification in each step of demonstrative knowledge,[1] so must there always be a fact of pure experience at the base of each judgment in the series. When we reach a conclusion by synthesizing judgments of various facets of something, even though we might lack a factual intuition that unifies the whole, a logical intuition that unifies and synthesizes all the relations is functioning. (Even the so-called three laws of thought[2] are a kind of inner intuition.) For example, in surmising from various observations that the earth is moving, one makes that judgment in accordance with the laws of logic grounded in a kind of intuition.

1. Nishida's note is "Locke, *An Essay Concerning Human Understanding*, bk.IV, ch.II, 7." In section 7 of chapter 2, Locke writes, "Now, in every step reason makes in demonstrative knowledge, there is an intuitive knowledge of that agreement or disagreement it seeks with the next intermediate idea, which it uses as a proof; since without the perception of such agreement or disagreement there is no knowledge produced. . . . By which it is plain, that every step in reasoning that produces knowledge has intuitive certainty." John Locke, *An Essay Concerning Human Understanding* (London: George Routledge and Sons Limited, n.d.), 435.

2. The three laws of thought are the law of identity, the law of contradiction, and the law of the excluded middle. The law of identity is expressed in the formula, "A is A"; each thing is what it is and as such can be a predicate for itself. The law of contradiction states that "A is not not-A," and logically this indicates that contradictory judgments cannot both be true. The law of the excluded middle is that "Everything is either A or not-A (and cannot be something in the middle)," which in part means that contradictory judgments cannot both be false and hence do not point to the truth of a third or middle judgment.

Thinking and pure experience traditionally have been considered totally different mental activities. But when we cast off dogma and consider this straightforwardly, we see that, as James said in "The World of Pure Experience," even the consciousness of relations is a kind of experience— so we realize that the activity of thinking constitutes a kind of pure experience.

We can distinguish perceptions and the mental images that constitute thinking by regarding the former as arising from the stimulation of nerve endings by external objects and the latter from stimuli in the cortex of the brain. Internally we rarely confuse perceptions with mental images, but when viewed in a purely psychological manner we cannot easily make a strict distinction between the two. The distinction between them is not absolute because it derives from their differing intensities and relations to other things. (In dreams and hallucinations we often confuse mental images with perceptions.) This distinction does not exist in the primordial consciousness; perceptions and mental images are only later distinguished on the basis of their relations to other things. Perception seems to be a simple event and thinking a complex process, but perception is not necessarily simple, for it too is a constitutive activity. And in its aspect of unity, thinking is a single activity that develops a certain unifying reality.

Let us discuss this further, as there may be objections to putting thinking in the same category as perceptual experience. People usually think that perceptual experiences are passive because the activity is completely unconscious and that thinking is active because the activity is completely conscious. But can we make such a clear-cut distinction? When developing and operating freely, thinking also bases itself almost entirely on unconscious attention. Contrary to what one might expect, thinking becomes conscious when its advance is hindered. That which advances thinking is not voluntary activity, for thinking develops on its own; only when we rid ourselves of the self and merge with the object of thought or the problem—when we lose ourselves in its midst—does the thinking activity emerge.

Thinking has its own laws. It functions of its own accord and does not follow our will. To merge with the object of thought—that is, to direct one's attention to it—is voluntary, but I think perception is the same in this respect: we are able to see what we want to see by freely turning our attention toward it. When compared with perception the unity in thinking seems looser and its transitions more conscious. Even this distinction, which we took earlier to be thinking's special feature, is relative. In the instant it shifts from one representation to the next, thinking, too, is unconscious, and as long as the unifying activity is actually functioning it must be unconscious. By the time we are conscious of this activity as an object, it already belongs to the past. The unifying activity of thinking is in this way completely outside the will.

When we think about a problem it seems that we can freely select from various lines of thought. This holds for perception as well. In a somewhat complex perception, we are free to direct our attention. Looking at a picture, for example, we can be attentive to its form or its colors. And although people contend that in perception we are moved from without and in thinking we move from within, the distinction between external and internal is relative. People make this distinction simply because the mental images that constitute the material of thinking change with relative ease and shift on their own.

Many people think that perception and thinking are completely different because perception is a consciousness of concrete facts whereas thinking is a consciousness of abstract relations. But we cannot be conscious of purely abstract relations. The movement of thinking occurs by virtue of certain concrete mental images, and without them it cannot take place. To prove, for example, that the sum of the angles of a triangle equals the sum of two right angles, we must depend on the mental image of a particular triangle. This thinking is not an independent consciousness divorced from such mental images, for it is a phenomenon that accompanies them. Gore explained that the relationship between a mental image and its meaning is identical to that between a stimulus and its response.[3] Thinking is the response of consciousness to a mental image, and the mental image is the first step in thinking: thinking and mental images are not separate things. A mental image, regardless of its type, never stands alone, for it inevitably appears in some relation to the whole of consciousness. This aspect of thinking is relational consciousness, and pure thinking is thinking in which this aspect is especially distinctive.

Given the relation between mental images and thinking, we must ask whether perception involves something similar to what we see in thinking. It always does, for like all phenomena of consciousness, perception is a systematic activity. The result of a perception is quite noticeable because it comes forth as will or movement, but in the case of a mental

3. Nishida's note is "Dewey, Studies in Logical Theory."

image thinking does not go beyond internal relations. In actual consciousness, then, a distinction holds between perceptions and mental images, but not between the concrete and abstract. Thinking is consciousness of actual relations among mental images, and, as previously discussed, from the standpoint of pure experience in the strict sense no distinction can be made between perceptions and mental images.

In the foregoing paragraphs, I argued from the perspective of psychology that even thinking is a kind of pure experience; but thinking is not simply a fact that occurs in an individual's consciousness—it possesses objective meaning. The primary function of thinking is to manifest truth. Although there is no true or false in pure experience as the intuition of one's own phenomena of consciousness, thinking does include a distinction between true and false. To clarify this, we must consider in detail the meaning of such terms as objectivity, reality, and truth. When we think critically, we realize that reality does not exist apart from the facts of pure experience and we can explain the character of these notions psychologically.

As stated earlier, consciousness derives meaning from its relations to other consciousnesses—meaning is determined by the system to which consciousness belongs. Identical consciousnesses yield different meanings by virtue of the different systems in which they participate. For example, when a mental image that is a consciousness of a certain meaning is viewed simply as it is with no relation to anything else, it is merely a fact of pure experience with no meaning whatsoever. Conversely, consider a perception that constitutes consciousness of a certain fact: though it possesses meaning by virtue of its relations with other things in the system of consciousness, in many cases this meaning is unconscious.

Which ideas are true and which false? We always believe that what is most powerful, greatest, and deepest in a system of consciousness is objective reality. Whatever fits with it we consider true, and whatever conflicts with it we consider false. We judge the correctness or error of perceptions from this perspective as well. Thus, in a given system a perception is correct when it fits well with the system's purposes; when it runs contrary to them, it is in error.

These systems of course contain a variety of meanings, so we might make the distinction that systems of perception are mainly practical, whereas systems of thinking are a matter of pure knowledge. My view, however, is that since the ultimate purpose of knowledge is practical, reason functions at the base of the will. Though I shall discuss this later in regard to the will, let me state here that even this distinction between the two systems is not absolute. Although they are equally activities of knowing, an association of ideas or memory is simply a relationship—or, more strongly, a unity—within an individual's consciousness, whereas thinking is trans-individual and general. This distinction derives from our limiting the scope of experience to the individual and our failure to arrive at the recognition that there is no individual person prior to pure experience. (Will is the lesser, and reason the profound, demand of the unity of consciousness.)

Up to this point we have compared thinking with pure experience. Despite our ordinary view of these as two completely different things, deeper reflection reveals a point of correspondence between them. To clarify their relation further, let us consider the origin, course, and outcome of thinking.

Probably everyone agrees that the primordial state of our consciousness and the immediate state of developing consciousness are at all times states of pure experience. The activity of reflective thinking arises secondarily out of this. If this is indeed the case, why does this activity arise? Consciousness, as stated earlier, is fundamentally a single system; its nature is to develop and complete itself. In the course of its development various conflicts and contradictions crop up in the system, and out of this emerges reflective thinking. But when viewed from a different angle, that which is contradictory and conflicted is the beginning of a still greater systematic development; it is the incomplete state of a greater unity. In both conduct and knowledge, for example, when our experience becomes complex and various associations arise to disturb the natural course of our experience, we become reflective. Behind this contradiction and conflict is a possible unity. In the midst of decision or the resolution of conflicts, then, the groundwork of a great unity has already been laid.

We never rest in the internal states of unity that arise from decisions or conflict resolution: decision is always accompanied by action. Likewise, even thought necessarily has some sort of practical meaning and must come forth in action. Both conduct and knowledge must arrive at the unity of pure experience.[4] The fact of pure experience in this regard is the alpha and omega of our thought, and thinking is the process by which a great system of consciousness develops and actualizes itself.

4. Consciousness, for Nishida, is a self-developing system. It originates in pure experience and develops itself through various conflicts and contradictions in terms of conduct and knowledge. It finally arrives at a unity in which pure experience is fully realized.

Viewed from within the great unity of consciousness, thinking is a wave on the surface of a great intuition. When we are troubled about some goal, for example, the unified consciousness that is the goal operates at all times as an intuitive fact behind our thinking. Accordingly, thinking does not possess a content or form different from pure experience. Though it may be profoundly great, thinking is simply an incomplete state of pure experience. From another angle, a truly pure experience is not passive, for it has a constitutive, universal aspect; pure experience includes thinking.

The notions of pure experience and thinking derive from two different views of what is fundamentally one and the same fact. If in line with Hegel's emphasis on the power of thinking we assume that the essence of thinking is not abstract but concrete, then thinking is nearly identical to pure experience in my sense of the expression, and pure experience is none other than thinking. From the perspective of concrete thinking, the universality of a concept is not what we usually say it is—that is, an abstraction of similar natures from something concrete. Rather, it is the unifying force of concrete facts. Hegel likewise writes that the universal is the soul of the concrete.[5]

Because pure experience is a systematic development, the unifying force that functions at its foundation is the universality of concepts; the development of experience corresponds to the advance of thinking; and the facts of pure experience are the self-actualization of the universal. Even in the case of sensations and associations of ideas, a concealed unifying activity operates in the background. In contrast, as noted before, when the unity in thinking functions, it is unconscious; only when the unity is abstracted and objectified does it appear as a different consciousness—but then the unifying activity has already been lost. If pure experience were simple or passive it would be opposed to thinking. But if pure experience means to know things just as they are, then simplicity or passivity are not characteristics of it—the truly direct state is constitutive and active.

We ordinarily think we know the universal through thinking and the individual through experience. But apart from the individual there is no universal. That which is truly universal is the concealed power behind the actualization of the individual; the universal is located within the individual as the power that causes the individual to develop. It is like

5. Nishida's note is "Hegel, *Wissenschaft der Logik,* III, S.37."

the seed of a plant. If the universal were something abstracted from an individual entity and stood in opposition to other particulars, it would after all be a particular, not a genuine universal; the universal would not hold a position above that of a particular but would have equal status. Take, for example, a colored triangle. From the standpoint of triangularity, the color is a particular characteristic, but from the standpoint of color, the triangularity is a particular characteristic. If universals were likewise this abstract and powerless they would not constitute the basis for inference or synthesis. The true universal at the base of the unity that is found in the activity of thinking therefore must be the concealed power that takes as its content the individual actuality. The universal and the individual differ only in that one is implicit and the other explicit; the individual is that which is determined by the universal.

When we consider the relation between the universal and the individual in this way, the logical distinction between thinking and experience disappears. Our present individual experience is actually in the process of development; it possesses a concealed power, which can be still more finely determined. In the case of sensation, for example, there may be room for further development through differentiation, and from this angle we can regard it as universal. Conversely, if we examine something universal at only one point of its development, we can deem it as individual. Usually, the only things we label as individual are those that are determined in time and space, but this type of determination is merely external. The true individual must be individual in its content—it must be something with unique characteristics. In the true individual something universal has reached the extreme limit of its development. What we ordinarily refer to as sensation or perception is a universal that is meager in content. And contrary to what one might think, a painter's intuition full of profound meaning is truly individual.

In all likelihood, a materialistic bias underlies the view that an individual is a merely material entity determined in time and space. From the standpoint of pure experience, we should compare experiences by means of their content. Even things like time and space are nothing more than forms that unify experiences according to content. The strength and clarity of a sense impression and its close relation with feeling and volition are probably the primary reasons for our thinking of sense impressions as individual. Yet even such a phenomenon as thought is never unrelated to feeling and volition. That which moves our feeling and volition powerfully is usually regarded as especially individual, for in contrast to knowledge, feeling and volition are our goal and are close to the culmination of the development of consciousness.

In summary, thinking and experience are identical. Although we can see a relative difference, there is no absolute distinction between them. I am not saying that thinking is merely individual and subjective. Pure experience can, as discussed earlier, transcend the individual person. Although it may sound strange, experience knows time, space, and the individual person and so it is beyond them. It is not that there is experience because there is an individual, but that there is an individual because there is experience. The individual's experience is simply a small, distinctive sphere of limited experience within true experience.

CHAPTER 3

Will

From the standpoint of pure experience I will now discuss the character of the will and clarify the relationship between knowing and willing. The will often takes action as its goal and accompanies it, but the will is a mental phenomenon that is distinct from external action, and action is not a necessary condition of the will. Even when circumstances in the external world are such that action does not occur, the will is still functioning. As psychologists say, we can will a movement simply by recollecting a past memory; if we direct our attention to the memory, the movement will follow naturally. From the standpoint of pure experience the movement itself is but a continuation of the sensation of movement in recollection. Further, when seen directly, it becomes clear that the goals of the will are actually facts that exist within consciousness; we will our own state at all times, and in the will there is no distinction between internal and external.

We tend to think of the will as some special power, but in fact it is nothing more than the experience of shifting from one mental image to another. To will something is to direct attention to it. We see this most clearly in so-called involuntary conduct. In the aforementioned perceptual train, for example, the shift of attention and the advance of the will correspond exactly. This does not mean that attention is limited to the will—its scope may be wider—but that the will usually exists as a state of attention vis-à-vis the system of movement representations. To put it differently, the will emerges when the system of attention occupies consciousness and we become one with it.

We might think that simply paying attention to a representation is different from seeing it as a goal of the will, but the difference lies in the system to which the representation belongs. All consciousness is systematic and no representation arises alone—it necessarily belongs to some system. Depending on the systems to which they belong, two identical representations can become an object of knowledge and a goal of the will. In recollecting a cup of water, for example, when the cup is associated simply with conditions in the external world it becomes an object of knowledge, but when it is associated with one's own movements it becomes a goal of the will. Goethe's notion that the unattainable stars in the heavens are beautiful[1] is related to the idea that that which does not enter the system of one's own movement representations cannot be a goal of the will.

It is a fact that all our desires arise through the recollection of past experiences. Desires are characterized by both strong feelings and sensations of tension. Regarding the former, the system of movement representations is based on what are for us the strongest life instincts; the latter are the muscular sensations accompanying movement. We cannot argue that just to recollect a movement is to will it, for at the time of

1. Mephistopheles says about Faust to God: "Forsooth, he serves you most peculiarly. / Unearthly are the fool's drink and his food; / The ferment drives him forth afar. / Though half aware of his insensate mood, / He asks of heaven every fairest star / And of the earth each highest zest, / And all things near and all things far / Can not appease his deeply troubled breast." *Goethe,* vol.47, 8. For Nishida, because we cannot reach the stars in the heavens we can not take them as goals of the will. Therefore, free from human volitional interest, they are simply beautiful.

recollection the movement representations have not yet occupied the whole of consciousness. It is only when they become purely one with it that the will immediately begins to act in a decisive manner.

What then is the difference between systems of movement representations and systems of representations in knowing? In the beginning of the development of consciousness there are no such distinctions. Originally, organisms perform various movements in order to preserve life. Because consciousness evolves in accordance with such instinctual movements, the primordial state is impulsive rather than perceptual. But because we can make various associations of ideas to the extent that experiences accumulate, two kinds of systems become possible: one is based on the center of perception and the other is based on the center of movement. No matter how much the two systems diverge, however, they do not completely differ in kind. Pure knowing in some respect possesses practical meaning, and pure will is based upon knowledge of some sort. Concrete mental phenomena are endowed with both aspects. Knowing and the will are simply two ways of referring to one phenomenon by separating the distinctive aspects. From this perspective on mental phenomena, perception is a kind of impulsive will and the will is a kind of recollection. Moreover, even the pure knowing involved in memory representations does not necessarily lack practical meaning. And the will, though often regarded as arising by chance, is actually based on some kind of stimulus. People may say that the will usually advances from within toward certain goals, but even perception can set its goal beforehand and then direct the sense organs toward it. Thinking is completely voluntary, whereas the impulsive will is thoroughly passive.

Accordingly, movement representations and knowledge representations are not completely different in kind, and the distinction between the will and knowing is merely relative. However weak, both the feelings of pleasure and pain and the sense of tension that are characteristic of the will inevitably accompany the activity of knowing. From a subjective perspective, knowledge can also be regarded as the development of an internal latent power. We can, as mentioned earlier, think of both the will and knowledge as systematic developments of a concealed reality.

When viewing the subject and object separately we make a distinction: in knowledge, we subordinate the subject to the object, whereas in the will, we subordinate the object to the subject. To discuss this in detail, we must clarify the nature of the subject and the object as well as their relationship, but knowledge and the will have a point in common. In the activity of knowledge, we first hold an assumption and then look at it in light of facts. No matter how empirical our research might be, we must first have assumptions. When an assumption is congruent with the so-called objects, we believe it is true; we feel we were able to know the truth. In the case of volitional movements, having a desire does not lead directly to decisive action on the part of the will; only when we have considered the desire in light of objective facts and have grasped the appropriate possibilities do we shift to performance. Hence we cannot say that in an act of knowledge we completely subordinate the subject to the object whereas in a volitional act we subordinate the object to the subject. A desire can be fulfilled only through congruence with the object. The farther the will recedes from the object, the more ineffective it becomes; the closer it approaches, the more effective it becomes.

When attempting to put a lofty goal divorced from actuality into action, we must consider various means and proceed step by step accordingly. To consider means in this manner is to seek harmony and accord with the object. If in the long run we fail to discover appropriate means, we have no recourse other than to alter the goal. On the other hand, when the goal is close to the given actuality, as in the habitual conduct of everyday life, the desire immediately turns into performance. In this case we do not function out of the subject; rather, we function out of the object.

Just as we do not completely subordinate the object to the subject in volition, we do not completely subordinate the subject to the object in knowledge. When our ideas constitute an objective truth—when it is known that our ideas follow the laws of reality and that objective reality operates according to them—have we not then been able to realize our ideal? Thinking is also a kind of apperceptive activity; it is an internal will based on a demand to know. Is not our being able to reach a goal of thinking therefore a kind of fulfillment of the will? The difference between volition and knowledge is that in volition we modify objective facts to accord with our ideal, whereas in knowledge we modify our ideal to accord with objective facts; one produces and the other discovers. But truth is not something we can produce—it is something in accordance with which we should think.

We must now ask whether truth ever exists totally separate from the subject? From the standpoint of pure experience, there is no such thing as an object divorced from the subject. Truth is that which has unified our experiential facts, and objective truth is the system of representations that is most effective and most integrating. To know the truth or to accord with it is to unify our experience; it is to proceed from a lesser to a greater unity. If we regard our authentic self as being this unifying activity, then to know the truth is to accord with this greater self, to actualize it. (As Hegel said, the goal of all learning is for spirit to know itself in all things of the universe.) As knowledge deepens, the activity of the self becomes greater, for that which was not the self now enters into the system of the self.

Because our thinking usually centers on individual demands, we feel ourselves to be passive in knowing, but if we relocate the center of consciousness in so-called rational demands, then we become active in knowing. As Spinoza said, knowledge is power.[2] We believe we can move our bodies freely by recalling past movement representations. But our bodies are made of matter, so they are no different from other material bodies. To know the change of an external thing through one's vision is the same as feeling the movement of one's own body through muscular sensation. Hence the "external world" refers both to our bodies and to other material things. Yet why do we think that we can freely control only our own bodies and not external objects? We usually consider movement representations to be both our mental images and the cause of movement in the external world. From the standpoint of pure experience, however, to say that we move the body by means of the movement representation is simply to recognize that a movement sensation accompanies a certain anticipatory movement representation. This is the same as the actualization of anticipated changes in the external world. In the state of primordial consciousness, the movement of one's own body and the movement of an external object are perhaps identical, and they come to be distinguished only as experience advances. That which occurs under specific conditions is regarded as a change in the external world and that which immediately complies with the anticipatory representation is regarded as one's own movement. Yet this distinction is not absolute, for slightly complicated movements do not comply directly with anticipatory representations. In this regard, the activity of the will distinctly approaches the activity of knowledge.

2. Following Francis Bacon earlier in the sixteenth century, Baruch Spinoza (1632–1697) maintained that "knowledge is power": the self-determining intellect is a type of efficient power (the efficient cause of its ideas) and human virtue is the activity of the intellect. David Bidney, *The Psychology and Ethics of Spinoza: A Study in the History and Logic of Ideas* (New York: Russell & Russell, 1962), 285.

In summary, if we regard a change in the external world as actually a change in our world of consciousness—that is, as a change within pure experience, and if we regard the presence and absence of conditions as differences in degree, then the fulfillment of knowledge and the fulfillment of the will turn out to be of the same character. Someone may argue that an anticipatory representation does not simply come before a willed movement but directly functions as the cause of the movement, whereas an anticipatory representation in our knowing does not constitute the cause of a change in the external world. But fundamentally causality is an invariable continuity of phenomena of consciousness. If for the sake of argument we were to posit the existence of an external world completely independent from consciousness, then a conscious anticipatory representation in volition could not be considered the cause of movement in the external world, for all we could say is that the two phenomena parallel each other. From this perspective, the relationship of the anticipatory representation in volition to movement is identical with the relationship of the anticipatory representation in knowledge to the external world. In actuality, an anticipatory representation in volition and the movement of the body do not accompany each other except under certain conditions.

We usually contend that the will is free. But what is this so-called freedom? Our desire essentially is something imparted to us—we cannot produce it freely. Only when we function according to a certain profound, imparted motive do we feel we are active and free. Conversely, when we function in opposition to such a motive, we feel compulsion. This is the true meaning of freedom. Freedom in this sense is synonymous with the systematic development of consciousness. In knowledge, too, we are free in the same way. We think we can freely desire anything, but that simply means that it is possible for us to desire. Actual desires are imparted at specific times. When a motive is developing, we might be able to predict the next desire, but otherwise we cannot know beforehand what the self will desire in the next instant. It is not so much that I produce desires, but that actualized motives are none other than me. People usually say that a transcendent self outside desire freely decides motives, but of course there is no such mystical power; and if decisions made by such a transcendent self did exist, they would be fortuitous and anything but free.

As we have noted, there is no absolute distinction between volition and knowledge. Any assumed distinction is but an arbitrary judgment imposed from without. As facts of pure experience, volition and knowledge are indistinguishable. Together they constitute a process through which a universal reality systematically actualizes itself. The culmination of their unity is truth, and at the same time this culmination is praxis. In the case of perceptual trains, knowledge and the will are still undivided—knowing is none other than acting. With the development of consciousness, because of conflict among various systems—which is an advance toward a still greater unity—one can distinguish between ideals and facts; the subjective and objective worlds diverge; and the idea arises that volition is a movement from the subject to the object whereas knowledge is a movement from the object to the subject. This distinction between willing and knowing arises when we separate the subject and the object and lose the unified state of pure experience.

Both desires in the will and ideas in knowing are states of disunity in which ideals separate from facts. Even an idea is a type of demand vis-à-vis objective facts, and so-called truth is an idea that fits the facts and ought to be actualized. Viewed in this way, truth is identical with a desire that matches facts and can be actualized. The distinction is simply that the former is universal whereas the latter is individual. The fulfillment of the will or the culmination of truth thus means that from a state of disunity one has arrived at the state of pure experience.

This approach to the fulfillment of the will is clear, but this approach to truth requires some explanation. There are various arguments about what truth is, but I think truth is that which comes closest to the most concrete facts of experience. Truth is sometimes said to be universal but if by this one means abstract commonality, then what one is designating is actually far removed from truth. The culmination of truth is the most concrete, direct facts that synthesize various facets of experience. These facts are the basis of truth, and truth is something abstracted and constructed out of them. Though truth lies in unity, the unity is not a unity of abstract concepts. True unity lies in direct facts. Perfect truth pertains to the individual person and is actual. Perfect truth therefore cannot be expressed in words, and such things as scientific truth cannot be considered perfect truth.

The standard of truth is not external, for it lies in our state of pure experience. To know the truth is to be congruent with this state. Even in abstract disciplines like mathematics, the foundational principles lie in our intuition, in direct experience. There are various classes of experience; when we include the consciousness of relations as experience, even such things as mathematical intuition constitute a kind of experience. If various direct experiences exist in this way, then one may wonder how we can determine their truth or falsehood. When two experiences are enveloped by a third, we can judge the two according to the third.

It is in the state of direct experience—when subject and object merge with each other and we are unable, even if we try, to doubt the single actuality of the universe—that we have conviction about truth. The activity of the will is an expression of this kind of direct experience; it is the establishment of the unity of consciousness. The expression of desire, like the expression of a representation, is simply a fact of direct experience. Arriving at a decision after a struggle between various desires, like making a judgment after various deliberations, is the establishment of an internal unity. Just as one's scientific conjectures are proven through experimentation, what becomes manifest when the will has been fulfilled in the external world is the most unified, direct experience, which has broken through the subject-object distinction. One might say that the unity within consciousness is free, whereas to achieve a unity with the external world we must accord with nature—but a unity of the internal world is not free, for all unities are imparted to us. And viewed from the perspective of pure experience, even distinctions between internal and external are relative.

The activity of the will is not merely a state of hope. Hope is a state of disunity in consciousness, a situation in which the fulfillment of the will is obstructed. The unity of consciousness is the state of the activity of the will. Regardless of the extent to which actuality is opposed to the self's true hope, when the will is satisfied with and purely one with that actuality, actuality is the fulfillment of the will. Conversely, however complete circumstances may be, when there are various hopes apart from the will and when actuality is in a state of disunity, the will is obstructed. The activity of the will and the denial of that activity are related to simplicity and nonsimplicity, to unity and disunity.

For example, I have a pen here. In the instant of seeing it, there is neither knowledge nor volition—there is just a single actuality. When various associations concerning it arise, the center of consciousness shifts, and when the original consciousness is objectified, it comes to be merely intellectual. In contrast, let us imagine that the associated idea arises that this pen is for writing letters. While this associated idea is still attached to the original consciousness as a fringe element, it is knowledge, but when the associative consciousness begins to stand on its own—when the center of consciousness has begun to shift toward it—it becomes a state of desire. Accordingly, when associative consciousness has become an increasingly independent actuality, it is the will and, in addition, one truly knows it.

I view any state in which the system of consciousness develops in actuality as the activity of the will. Even in thinking, the focusing of attention on a problem and the seeking of a solution is a form of the will. In contrast, consider the act of drinking tea or *sake*: if there is simply the actuality of drinking, then this is an instance of the will; but if a consciousness that tries to taste the flavor arises and becomes central, we have knowledge. In this example, the consciousness that tastes the flavor is the will. In comparison with ordinary knowing, the will is a more fundamental system of consciousness; it is the center of unity. The distinction between knowledge and volition does not lie in the content of consciousness—it is determined by their place within that system.

At first glance, reason and desire may seem mutually opposed, but I think that in actuality both have the same character and differ only in magnitude and depth. What we call the demands of reason are actually demands for a greater unity; they are demands of the universal system of consciousness that transcends the individual person, and they can even be seen as the manifestation of a great, trans-individual will. The sphere of consciousness is never limited to the individual person, for the individual is no more than a small system within consciousness. We usually regard as central the small system that takes bodily existence for its nucleus, but if we regard the great system of consciousness as central, then this great system is the self, and its development is the fulfillment of that self's will. This is what we find in people of religion, scholars, and artists.

The laws of reason, which say, "It must be like this," and the tendency of the will, which simply says, "I want it to be like this," appear to be completely different, but when we consider them carefully we see that they share the same foundation. The unifying activity of the will functions at the base of all reason and laws. As Schiller and others have argued, even axioms originally developed out of practical need; in their mode of origination, they do not differ from our hopes.[3] Although the

---

3. Nishida's note is "Sturt, *Personal Idealism*, p.92." In his essay "Axioms as Postulates," Schiller writes that postulates "may rise from the crudest cravings of individual caprice to universal desires of human emotions." Henry Cecil Sturt, ed., *Personal Idealism: Philosophical Essays by Eight Members of the University of Oxford* (London: Macmillan, 1902), 92.

tendency of our will seems not to accord with laws, it is governed by necessary laws, and it is the unity of an individual's consciousness. Reason and the will are laws of the development of the system of consciousness, and only the scope of their efficacy differs.

Some people draw a distinction between the will and reason because the will is blind. But we cannot explain a direct fact; we cannot explain the intuitive principles at the base of reason. To explain is to be able to include other things in a single system. That which is the very nucleus of a unity cannot be explained; thus, it is blind.[4]

4. Because the nucleus of a unity—the intuitive principles at the base of reason—is unexplainable, Nishida says it is blind, just as the will is said to be blind.

CHAPTER 4

Intellectual Intuition

Intellectual intuition (*intellektuelle Anschauung*) is an intuition of ideal, usually trans-experiential things. It intuits that which can be known dialectically. Examples of this are found in the intuition of artists and people of religion. With respect to the process of intuiting, intellectual intuition is identical to ordinary perception, but with respect to content, intellectual intuition is far richer and more profound.

Some think of intellectual intuition as a kind of special mystical ability. Others think of it as an idle fancy cut off from experiential facts. I believe, however, that it is the same as ordinary perception and that the two cannot be clearly demarcated. Ordinary perception is never purely simple, for it contains ideal elements and is compositional. Though I am presently looking at something, I do not see it just as it is in the present; I see it as mediated in an explanatory manner through the force of past experience.

The ideal elements in perception are not associated ideas added from the outside—they are elements that structure a perception and a perception is transformed by them. The ideal elements hidden at the base of a perception can become extremely rich and profound, and they vary according to the talents or degrees of experiential development in people. With the advance of experience, both that which at first could not be experienced and that which could be only gradually known dialectically come to appear as intuitional facts. One cannot determine the scope of intuition by taking one's own present experience as the yardstick. Though there are things that I cannot intuit now, this does not mean that nobody can. It is said that when Mozart composed music, including his long pieces, he could discern the whole at once, like a picture or a statue. The ideal elements are not simply built in increments quantitatively, but become qualitatively profound. The culmination of this profundity is found in the intuition possessed by a person of religion who, through human love, can intuit the oneness of self and other. Whether a person's extraordinary intuition is simply an idle fancy or truly an objectively real intuition hinges on its relation to other things, on its effects. In terms of direct experience, an idle fancy and a genuine intuition have the same essential quality; there is only a quantitative difference in the scope of their unities.

Some people think that an intellectual intuition differs from ordinary perception in that it transcends space, time, and the individual person and directly penetrates the true nature of reality. But from the standpoint of pure experience in the strict sense, experience is not bound to such forms as time, space, and individual persons; rather, these discriminations derive from an intuition that transcends them. Furthermore, with respect to seeing reality directly, there is no distinction between subject and object in any state of direct experience—one encounters reality face to face. This is not limited to an individual intellectual intuition; Schelling's "identity" (*Identität*)[1] is a state of direct experience. The distinction be-

---

1. In a later development of his thought, Schelling sets forth the identity of the subjective and objective, the ideal and real, the infinite and finite, and the unconscious and conscious. This identity, or "point of indifference," is the Absolute, and it is only through intellectual intuition at the base of philosophical reflection that one grasps the Absolute.

tween subject and object is a relative form that arises when one has lost the unity of experience, and to regard subject and object as mutually independent realities is an arbitrary view.

Schopenhauer's pure intuition without will is not a special ability of a genius, but rather our most natural, unified state of consciousness. An innocent baby's intuitions fall into this category. Intellectual intuition is just that which deepens and enlarges our state of pure experience; it is the manifestation of a great unity in the systematic development of consciousness. When a scholar achieves a new idea, the moral person a new motive, the artist a new ideal, the religious person a new awakening, such a unity is manifesting itself. (These achievements are all rooted in mystical intuition.) If our consciousness were simply sensory, it would go no farther than being a state of ordinary perceptual intuition. But an idealistic spirit seeks an unlimited unity, which is provided in the form of intellectual intuition. Intellectual intuition, like perception, is the most unified state of consciousness.

Just as ordinary perception is considered merely passive, so is intellectual intuition considered a state of passive contemplation; however, a true intellectual intuition is the unifying activity in pure experience. It is a grasp of life, like having the knack of an art or, more profoundly, the aesthetic spirit. For example, when inspiration arises in a painter and the brush moves spontaneously, a unifying reality is operating behind this complex activity. Its transitions are not unconscious, for they are the development and completion of a single thing.

Intellectual intuition, the discernment of this single reality, can be found not only in the fine arts but in all of our disciplined behavior; it is an extremely ordinary phenomenon. Mainstream psychologists may argue that it is only a habit or an organic activity, but from the standpoint of pure experience it is actually the state of oneness of subject and object, a fusion of knowing and willing. In the mutual forgetting of the self and the object, the object does not move the self and the self does not move the object. There is simply one world, one scene. Intellectual intuition sounds like a subjective activity, but actually it is a state that has transcended subject and object. In fact, the opposition of subject and object comes into being by means of this unity, and things like artistic inspiration attain to it.

Intellectual intuition is not an intuition of an abstract universality apart from facts. Though the spirit of a painting may differ from the individual things depicted, it is not divorced from them. True universality and individuality are not opposed to each other. We can express the true universal through the determination of individuality. Each of the artist's exquisite brush strokes expresses the true meaning of the whole.

Intellectual intuition thus underlies thinking. Thinking is a type of system, and at its base there must be an intuition of unity. As James said in "The Stream of Thought" regarding the consciousness that "the pack of cards is on the table," when we become conscious of the subject, the predicate is implied, and when we become conscious of the predicate, the subject is implied.[2] At the base of that consciousness, a single intuition is essentially identical to having the knack of an art. Stated broadly, a vast intuition functions behind such profound thought as the philosophies of Plato and Spinoza. In thought, a genius's intuition differs not in quality but in degree from ordinary thinking, and it is simply a new, profound intuition of unity.

Intuition lies at the base of all relations, and relations are established by means of it. However far and wide we extend our thought, we cannot go beyond basic intuition, for thought is established upon it. Thought cannot be explained exhaustively, for at its base exists an unexplainable intuiting upon which all proof is constructed. A certain mystical reality is always hidden at the base of thought, and this pertains even to the axioms of geometry. It is often said that thought can be explained but intuition cannot. The word "explanation" simply indicates the ability to return to the fundamental intuition. The intuiting that lies at the foundation of thought becomes the basis of explanation and is at the same time the power of thinking, not simply a static form of thought.

Intellectual intuition functions not only at the base of thinking but also at the base of the will. The will is established through this intuition because to will something is to intuit the oneness of subject and object. The advance of the will is the development and completion of this intuitional unity. From beginning to end, intuition functions at the base of the will, and the completion of intuitional unity constitutes the fulfillment of the will. Because this intuition is operative, we feel that the self functions in the will. The self does not exist apart from this intuition, for the true self is this unifying intuition. From this perspective, what

2. James writes that the various parts of the time-based statement "melt into each other like dissolving views, and no two of them feel the object just alike, but each feels the total object in a unitary undivided way." William James, "The Stream of Thought," in *The Principles of Psychology*, vol.1 (New York: Henry Holt, 1890), 279.

the ancients spoke of as acting from morning to night without acting we might call a stillness in motion, a doing of non-doing. In this way we transcend both knowledge and the will, and in the intuition at their base we can discover their oneness.

True religious awakening is neither an abstract knowledge based in thinking nor a blind feeling. In this awakening we realize with our whole being the profound unity at the base of knowledge and the will. It is a kind of intellectual intuition, a deep grasp of life. The sword of logic cannot penetrate it and desire cannot move it. This awakening is the basis of all truth and contentment. Though their forms vary, all religions necessarily contain this fundamental intuition at their bases. And religion must exist at the base of learning and morality, which comes into being because of religion.

PART II

Reality

CHAPTER 5

The Starting Point
of the Inquiry

Philosophical views of the world and of human life relate closely to the practical demands of morality and religion, which dictate how people should act and where they can find peace of mind. People are never satisfied with intellectual convictions and practical demands that contradict each other. Those with high spiritual demands fail to find satisfaction in materialism, and those who believe in materialism come to harbor doubts about spiritual demands. Fundamentally, truth is singular. Intellectual truth and practical truth must be one and the same. Those who think deeply or are genuinely serious inevitably seek congruence between knowledge and the practical realm of feeling and willing. We must now investigate what we ought to do and where we ought to find peace of mind, but this calls first for clarification of the nature of the universe, human life, and true reality.

The Indian religio-philosophical tradition, which provides the most highly developed congruence of philosophy and religion, holds that knowledge is good and delusion is evil. The fundamental reality of the universe is Brahman, which is our soul, our Ātman. Knowledge of this identity of Brahman and Ātman is the culmination of Indian philosophy and religion. Christianity was entirely practical at its inception, but because the human mind insistently demands intellectual satisfaction, Christian philosophy was developed in the Middle Ages. In the Chinese tradition, the system of morality at first lacked philosophical elaboration, but since the Sung period this dimension has predominated. Such historical trends in the Indian, Christian, and Chinese traditions attest to the basic human demand for congruence between our knowledge and our feeling and will.

In classical Western philosophy beginning with Socrates and Plato, didactic goals were central, whereas in modern times knowledge has assumed a prominent position, making the unity of the intellectual and the emotional-volitional aspects more difficult. In fact, the two dimensions now tend to diverge, and this in no way satisfies the fundamental demands of the human mind.

To understand true reality and to know the true nature of the universe and human life, we must discard all artificial assumptions, doubt whatever can be doubted, and proceed on the basis of direct and indubitable knowledge. From the perspective of common sense, we think that things exist in the external world apart from consciousness and that in the back of consciousness there is something called the mind, which performs various functions. Our assumption that mind and matter exist independently constitutes the basis of our conduct and is itself based on the demands posed by our thinking. This assumption leaves much room for doubt. Science, which does not take the most profound explanation of reality as its goal, is constructed on such hypothetical knowledge. But insufficiently critical thinking is also found in philosophy, which does take that explanation as its goal. Many philosophers base their thinking on existing assumptions and hence fail to engage in penetrating doubt.

The independent existence of mind and matter is generally considered an intuitive fact, but on reflection we realize that this clearly is not the case. What is the desk before me right now? Its color and shape are sensations of the eye; the feeling of resistance when I touch it is a sen-

sation of the hand. The form, size, position, and movement of a thing—
that which we intuit—are not the objective state of the thing in itself.
To intuit things in themselves apart from our consciousness is impossible.
This holds true for our minds as well. What we know is not the mind
itself but the *activity* of knowing, feeling, and willing. When viewed
psychologically, that which we think of as a self functioning through time
is nothing more than the continuation of a sensation or feeling; the mind
and matter that we take to be intuitive facts are merely unchanging com-
binations of similar phenomena of consciousness. We are led to believe
in the existence of mind and matter by the requirements of the law of
causality. But can we infer existence apart from consciousness by this
law? Let us now address this question.

What is direct knowledge that we cannot even begin to doubt? It is
knowledge of facts in our intuitive experience, knowledge of phenomena
of consciousness. A present phenomenon of consciousness and our being
conscious of it are identical; they cannot be divided into subject and
object. Since facts are not separated even a hair's breadth from knowing,
we cannot doubt this knowledge. Of course we can err when we judge
or recollect a phenomenon of consciousness, but at such a time we are
no longer engaged in intuition, for we have shifted to inference. The
later consciousness—which is engaged in judgment or recollection—and
the original consciousness are different phenomena of consciousness:
intuition is not the judging of the original consciousness by the later
one, but simply knowledge of facts just as they are. Accordingly, in intuition, erring or not erring is out of the question. All of our knowledge
must be constructed upon such intuitive experience.

Philosophy returns to such direct knowledge whenever it rids itself of
all existing assumptions and seeks anew a firm base. Bacon, at the dawn
of modern philosophy, considered experience the basis of all knowledge;
Descartes took as his philosophical starting point the proposition "I
think, therefore I am" (*cogito ergo sum*) and considered anything equally
clear to be truth. Nevertheless, experience in Bacon's framework was not
pure experience but experience accompanied by the arbitrary assumption
that we are able, by means of it, to intuit facts outside of consciousness.
And when Descartes said, "I think, therefore I am," his statement was
no longer a fact of immediate experience, for he was already inferring "I
am." Moreover, to hold that clear thinking can know noumena is an
arbitrary assumption; Kant and philosophers after him did not accept
this assumption as an indubitable truth. Accordingly, what I term direct

knowledge consists of the intuitive facts that are discerned when we abandon all such arbitrary assumptions. If I were to follow the lead of Hegel and succeeding historians of philosophy and to assume that Descartes's "I think, therefore I am" is not an inference but an expression of the intuitive certainty that links reality and thinking, then of course Descartes's starting point would be the same as mine.)

Some people regard not direct experience (as the intuition of facts in consciousness) but thinking as the starting point and most certain standard for knowledge. They draw a distinction between the noumenal and phenomenal aspects of things and argue that intuitively experienced facts are phenomena and that only through the activity of thinking can we clarify noumena. In common sense and science intuitive experience is not completely rejected, but certain kinds of experiential facts are considered true and other kinds false. For example, the sun, moon, and other celestial bodies appear to be quite small though they are actually immense; they seem to move though it is actually the earth that moves. To think that they are small or moving is to make inferences about experiential facts on the basis of other experiential facts that arise under different conditions. Each of the facts is indisputable within its own set of conditions—we must consider why it is that one of the intuitive facts is considered to be true and the other false. Such thoughts arise because that which is perceived through the sense of touch[1] is considered to be the true aspect of things, for touch, compared with the other senses, is universal and the most important in practice. But this view, upon reflection, lacks coherence.

A certain school of philosophy claims that experiential facts are the phenomenal aspect of things and that the noumenal aspect can be known only through thinking. If for the sake of argument we assume the existence of trans-experiential realities, how can they be known through thinking? No one can deny that the activity of thinking is a phenomenon of consciousness, and if we assume that experiential facts do not get at the noumenal aspect of things, then thinking cannot enable us to know it, either. Some people take the universality and necessity of thinking as

1. The original Japanese text is unclear here. "Such thoughts" appears to indicate the ideas concerning the sun, moon and so forth, but if this is the case then the term *shokkaku*, the sense of touch, seems unrelated to the observation of size and motion. Though the various printings of *An Inquiry into the Good* all have *shokkaku* here, there is a chance that Nishida intended to write *shikaku*, the sense of sight, which seems more appropriate in this context.

the standard for knowing true reality, but these qualities are a type of feeling intuited in consciousness; they, too, are facts of consciousness.

The standpoint that all sensory knowledge is misleading and that we can know the true nature of things only through thinking begins with the Eleatics[2] and reaches its peak with Plato. In modern philosophy, Cartesians believe that the true nature of reality can be known by clear thinking.

Thinking and intuition are usually considered to be totally different activities, but when we view them as facts of consciousness we realize that they are the same kind of activity. Many people hold that intuition and experience are purely passive activities in which we realize individual things just as they are irrespective of other things; in contrast, they regard thinking as an active function that compares and judges things and determines their relations. When we survey the range of actual activities of consciousness, however, we find no totally passive activity. Intuition is a direct judgment, and for this reason I stated before that intuition is the starting point of knowledge that is free from arbitrary assumptions.

"Intuition" thus does not refer simply to the activity of sensation. At the base of thinking there is always a certain unifying reality that we can know only through intuition. Judgment arises from the analysis of this intuition.

2. This school of Greek thinkers in Elea included Parmenides and Zeno, in the 6th and 5th centuries B.C.E.

CHAPTER 6

Phenomena
of Consciousness Are
the Sole Reality

From the perspective of direct knowledge that is free from all assumptions, reality consists only of phenomena of our consciousness, namely, the facts of direct experience. Any other notion of reality is simply an assumption generated by the demands of thinking. Because the activity of thinking does not go beyond the scope of the phenomena of consciousness, it possesses no mystical ability to intuit a reality above and beyond experience. Assumptions regarding such a reality are abstract concepts formulated so that thinking can systematically organize the facts of direct experience.

Highly critical thinking, which discards all arbitrary assumptions and starts from the most certain, direct knowledge, and thinking that assumes a reality outside the facts of direct experience are in no way compatible. Even such great philosophers as Locke and Kant fail to escape the contradiction between these two kinds of thinking. I intend to abandon all hypothetical thought and to engage in what I call critical thought. When we survey the history of philosophy, we see that Berkeley and Fichte also take this approach.

A phenomenon of consciousness is usually regarded as something that accompanies the animal nervous system in the realm of material objects. But reflection reveals that the most direct, primordial facts are actually phenomena of consciousness, not material phenomena. Even the body is simply a single part of the whole that consists of one's phenomena of consciousness, for it is not that consciousness is within the body, but that the body is within consciousness. To say that phenomena of consciousness accompany stimulation to nerve centers means that one sort of phenomenon of consciousness necessarily occurs together with another. Assuming we can know phenomena in the brain directly, the relation between phenomena of consciousness and the stimulation of the brain is identical to the relation between what one senses in the ear as sound and what one senses in the eye or the hand as the vibration of a string.

We believe that there are two types of experiential facts—phenomena of consciousness and phenomena of matter—but actually there is only one: phenomena of consciousness. Material phenomena are abstractions from phenomena of consciousness that are common to us all and possess an unchanging relation to each other.

People usually think that a noumenon with its fixed qualities exists independently of consciousness and that a phenomenon of consciousness is a phenomenon that arises merely on the basis of the noumenon. Yet what is the nature of such a fixed entity independent of consciousness? We cannot grasp the qualities of a *thing-in-itself* completely divorced from phenomena of consciousness—all we can say is that the thing-in-itself is a certain unknowable entity that under specific conditions gives rise to a specific phenomenon. Expressed differently, the noumenon is something we imagine because of the demands of our thinking. Why must thinking assume the existence of such a thing? This assumption is based on the fact that similar phenomena of consciousness always arise in a certain combination. This is the true meaning of what we call a "thing." From the perspective of pure experience, the unchanging combination of phenomena of consciousness is the fundamental fact, and the existence of the thing is simply an assumption made for the sake of explanation.

Materialists consider the existence of matter an indubitable, self-evident fact, and from this starting point they attempt to explain mental phenomena as well. With reflection, though, we see that their approach puts the cart before the horse. From the perspective of pure experience, there are no independent, self-sufficient facts apart from our phenomena of consciousness; as Berkeley said, "Esse est percipi" (to be is to be perceived). Our world consists of the facts called phenomena of consciousness, and all of the various philosophical and scientific systems are no more than explanations of these facts.

Some people might misunderstand "phenomena of consciousness" as indicating that the only existing thing is the mind, which is separated from matter. The gist of my argument is that true reality is neither a phenomenon of consciousness nor a material phenomenon. Even "esse est percipi" diverges from my view. Direct reality is not something passive—it is an independent, self-sufficient activity. Hence we should say, "To be is to act."

Deep reflection inevitably brings us to this conclusion, which, at a glance, runs contrary to common sense. When we attempt to explain the phenomena of the universe by means of it, we encounter a variety of difficult issues. Many of these issues, however, derive not from adherence to the standpoint of pure experience but from dogmatic assumptions appended to it.

One issue we encounter is that of possible solipsism. In taking only the phenomena of consciousness to be reality, do we not fall into the view that the whole world is simply our ideas? Even if we can avoid solipsism, if our consciousnesses are realities independent of each other, how can we explain their relations? That consciousness must be someone's consciousness simply means that consciousness must have a unity. The idea that there must be a possessor of consciousness above and beyond this unity is an arbitrary assumption. The activity of this unity—apperception—is a matter of similar ideas and feelings constituting a central hub and as such unifying consciousness. From the standpoint of pure experience, this unity of consciousness never entails absolute distinctions between itself and other such unities of consciousness. If we acknowledge that my consciousnesses of yesterday and today are independent and at the same time one consciousness in that they both belong to the same system, then we can recognize the same relationship between one's own consciousness and that of others.

The entire content of our thought and feeling is general. Even if people are separated by thousands of years or thousands of miles, thought and feeling can be communicated between them. For instance, a mathematical principle is the same whenever, wherever, and by whomever it is thought. A great person influences many people, unites them, and holds sway over them by means of their common spirit; at such time the spirit of the people is a unity.

The second issue that arises when we regard the phenomena of consciousness as the sole reality is this: assuming that phenomena of consciousness are not fixed things but a succession of constantly changing events, from where do they arise and to where do they go? This issue arises from the law of causality, which dictates that there must be a cause-effect relationship between things, so let us examine the demands of this law.

People usually think that the law of causality requires the existence of a fixed thing-in-itself behind a phenomenon, but this view is mistaken. As Hume said, the correct meaning of the law of causality is that in the arising of a certain phenomenon there is of necessity a particular phenomenon that precedes it, and that this does not require the existence of something above and beyond the phenomenon. For one phenomenon to give rise to another does not mean that the latter phenomenon was included in the former or that something other than the former was hidden and then revealed. Rather, it means that when certain sufficient conditions (causes) are provided, a certain phenomenon (the result) will necessarily occur. Prior to the provision of the conditions, the accompanying phenomenon, that is, the result, does not exist anywhere. For example, before we start a fire by striking a flint, the fire does not exist anywhere. It might be argued that a "power" starts the fire, but as we saw before, "power" or "thing" is an assumption made for the sake of explanation; as far as we know directly, there is only a specific phenomenon that is quite different from fire. That a specific phenomenon accompanies another is the fundamental fact given directly to us, and contrary to expectation, the requirements of the law of causality are based on this fact. The idea that the directly given fact and the law of causality contradict each other results from a misunderstanding of the law.[1]

The law of causality is thus a habit of thinking that derives from changes in our phenomena of consciousness. This is evident when we try to explain the universe as a whole by means of this law and fall into

---

1. That is, it results from the view that the law demands the existence of something above and beyond the given phenomenon.

self-contradiction. For example, the law of causality demands a beginning to the world. And if we decide upon a certain point as the beginning, the law of causality then calls for the cause of that point, and in this it reveals its own imperfection.

The third and final issue concerning phenomena of consciousness as the sole reality is the claim of the law of causality that being does not emerge from nothingness. When we assert that "there are no things"— from the perspective of intuition that transcends the distinction between subject and object—a consciousness of nothingness lies behind our assertion. Nothingness is not merely a word: its concrete meaning indicates the lack of certain qualities and also the possession of certain positive qualities (just as, psychologically, the color black is, like other colors, one type of sensation). When being is regarded as arising from nothingness in the physical world, the nothingness, as a fact of consciousness, is not true nothingness but a particular moment in the development of consciousness. In consciousness, how can being arise from nothingness? Consciousness is not affected by the quantitative limitations of time, place, and force, thus it is not controlled by the mechanical law of causality. In fact, such forms as time, place, and force are established upon the unity of consciousness. Consciousness is entirely qualitative, and in it a concealed "one" develops itself. Consciousness is what Hegel calls *das Unendliche*.[2]

For this reason, the sensation of just one color includes unlimited differences. As our consciousness becomes more precise, we come to sense unlimited variations of that one color. The discriminations in sensation that we possess at present in all likelihood have evolved through differentiation. Wilhelm Wundt discusses the qualities of sensations as existing in different gradations,[3] and it is because the qualities of sensation come forth through the division of single, universal entity that there can be such a system as his.

2. This term indicates that finite human consciousness is a part of the dialectical process of Absolute Spirit, which is infinite and eternal.

3. Nishida's note is, "Wundt, *Grundriss der Psychologie*, §5." Wundt writes that "every quality may, indeed, be so arranged in a definite continuity that it is possible to pass uninterruptedly from a given point to any other points in the same quality. But the various continuities of different qualities, which we may call *systems of quality*, exhibit differences both in the variety of possible gradations, and in the number of directions of gradation. In these two respects, we may distinguish, on the one hand, *homogeneous* and *complex*, on the other, *one-dimensional, two-dimensional, and many-dimensional* systems of quality." Wundt, *Outlines of Psychology*, 31–32.

CHAPTER 7

The True Features
of Reality

What is immediate reality before we have added the fabrications of think-ing? In other words, what is a fact of truly pure experience? At the time of pure experience, there is still no opposition between subject and object and no separation of knowledge, feeling, and volition; there is only an independent, self-sufficient, pure activity.

Intellectualist psychologists regard sensations and ideas as the requi-site elements of mental phenomena and hold that all mental phenomena are constituted by their union. From this perspective, they construe a fact of pure experience to be the most passive state of consciousness, namely, sensation. But this approach confuses the results of academic analysis with the facts of direct experience. In facts of direct experience, there is no pure sensation. What we term pure sensation is already a simple perception, but no matter how simple, perception is not at all passive: it necessarily includes active—constructive—elements (This is obvious when we consider examples of spatial perception.)

The characterization of pure experience as active becomes clearer when we examine such complex cognitive activities as association and thinking. Though association is usually deemed passive, the direction of the linkage of ideas in association is determined not only by circumstances in the external world, but also by the internal qualities of consciousness. Association and thinking thus differ only in degree. Moreover, people divide the phenomena of consciousness into knowledge, but in actuality we do not find these three types of phenomena. In fact, each and every phenomenon of consciousness possesses all three aspects. (For instance, although academic research is considered a purely intellectual activity, it can never exist apart from feeling and the will.) Of these three aspects the will is the most fundamental form of consciousness. As voluntarist psychologists assert, our consciousness is always active: it begins with an impulse and ends with the will. However simple, the most direct phenomena of consciousness take the form of the will—that is, the will is a fact of pure experience.

In the past, psychology was primarily intellectualist, although in recent times voluntarism has gradually come to the fore, with exponents like Wilhelm Wundt. From the newer perspective, consciousness is always constructive no matter how simple it may be. The contrasts in its content are necessary for its establishment—if there were truly simple consciousness, it would immediately become unconscious.

In pure experience, our thinking, feeling, and willing are still undivided; there is a single activity, with no opposition between subject and object. Such opposition arises from the demands of thinking, so it is not a fact of direct experience. In direct experience there is only an independent, self-sufficient event, with neither a subject that sees nor an object that is seen. Just like when we become enraptured by exquisite music, forget ourselves and everything around us, and experience the universe as one melodious sound, true reality presents itself in the moment of direct experience. Should the thought arise that the music is the vibration of air or that one is listening to music, at that point one has already separated oneself from true reality because that thought derives from reflection and thinking divorced from the true state of the reality of the music.

It is usually thought that subject and object are realities that can exist independently of each other and that phenomena of consciousness arise through their activity, which leads to the idea that there are two realities: mind and matter. This is a total mistake. The notions of subject and object derive from two different ways of looking at a single fact, as does the distinction between mind and matter. But these dichotomies are not inherent in the fact itself. As a concrete fact, a flower is not at all like the purely material flower of scientists; it is pleasing, with a beauty of color, shape, and scent. Heine[1] gazed at the stars in a quiet night sky and called them golden tacks in the azure. Though astronomers would laugh at his words as the folly of a poet, the true nature of stars may very well be expressed in his phrase.

In the independent, self-sufficient true reality prior to the separation of subject and object, our knowledge, feeling, and volition are one. Contrary to popular belief, true reality is not the subject matter of dispassionate knowledge; it is established through our feeling and willing. It is not simply an existence but something with meaning. If we were to remove our feelings and the will from this world of actuality, it would no longer be a concrete fact—it would become an abstract concept. The world described by physicists, like a line without width and a plane without thickness, is not something that actually exists. In this respect, it is the artist, not the scholar, who arrives at the true nature of reality. Each and every thing we see or hear contains our individuality. Though we might speak of identical consciousness, our consciousnesses are not truly the same. When viewing a cow, for example, farmers, zoologists, and artists have different mental images. Depending on one's feeling at the moment, the same scenery can appear resplendently beautiful or depressingly gloomy. Buddhist thought holds that according to one's mood the world becomes either heaven or hell. Thus our world is constructed upon our feeling and volition. However much we talk about the objective world as the subject matter of pure knowledge, it cannot escape its relation to our feelings.

People think that the world seen scientifically is most objective in that it exists independently of our feeling and volition. But it is in no way divorced from the demands of feeling and the will because scientific inquiry derives from actual demands in our struggle for survival. As

---

1. Heinrich Heine (1797–1856) was a German poet and critic who was heavily influenced by German romanticism.

especially Jerusalem has said, the idea that a power in the external world performs various activities—this idea being the fundamental principle of the scientific world view—is generated by analogical inference from one's will.[2] Ancient explanations of things in the universe were anthropomorphic, and they are the springboard from which contemporary scientific explanations developed.

Taking the distinction between subject and object as fundamental, some think that objective elements are included only in knowledge and that idiosyncratic, subjective events constitute feeling and volition. This view is mistaken in its basic assumptions. If we argue that phenomena arise by means of the mutual activity of subject and object, then even such content of knowledge as color or form can be seen as subjective or individual. If we argue further that there is a quality in the external world that gives rise to feeling and volition, then they come to possess an objective base, and it is therefore an error to say they are totally individual. Our feeling and volition allow for communication and sympathy between individuals; they have a trans-individual element.

Because we think that such emotional and volitional entities as joy, anger, love, and desire arise in individual people, we also think that feeling and the will are purely individual. Yet it is not that the individual possesses feeling and the will, but rather that feeling and the will create the individual. Feeling and the will are facts of direct experience.

The anthropomorphic explanation of the myriad things in the universe is the way of explanation used by ancient people and naive children in all eras. Although scientists might laugh it away—indeed, it is infantile—from a certain perspective this is the true way of explaining reality. A scientist's way of explanation is slanted toward just one aspect of knowledge, whereas in a complete explanation of reality we must satisfy intellectual demands as well as the demands of feeling and the will.

To the Greeks, all of nature was alive. Thunder and lightning were the wrath of Zeus on Mount Olympus, the voice of the cuckoo was Philamela's lament of the past.[3] To the natural eye of a Greek, the true meaning of the present appeared just as it was. Contemporary art, religion, and philosophy all strive to express this true meaning.

2. Nishida's note is "K.W. Jerusalem, *Einleitung in die Philosophie,* 6, Aufl. §27."

3. Nishida's note is "Friedrich Schiller, *Die Götter Griechenlands.*" Schiller's poem, "The Gods of Greece," includes the verse: "Yonder Laurel once imploring wound, / Tantal's daughter slumbers in this stone; / From yon rush rose Syrinx' mournful sound, / From this thicket, Philomela's moan." *Schiller's Works,* vol.1, ed. J.G. Fischer (Philadelphia: George Barrie, 1883), 36.

CHAPTER 8

True Reality
Constantly Has the Same
Formative Mode

The state of consciousness in which subject and object have dissolved into the union of thinking, feeling, and willing is true reality. Independent, self-sufficient true reality manifests itself in the form of this union. We must realize the true state of this reality with our entire being rather than reflect on it, analyze it, or express it in words. Because various types of discriminative knowledge derive from reflection on this reality, let us consider the formative mode in which it establishes itself and clarify how various discriminations arise from it.

True reality, like the true meaning of art, is not something that can be transmitted from one person to another. All we can transmit is an abstract shell. We may think that by means of the same language we understand the same thing, but to some extent the content necessarily differs.

Independent true reality complete unto itself is established in the same mode in all things: the whole first appears implicitly, and from it the content develops through differentiation; when that development ends, the whole of the reality[1] is actualized and completed—one entity has developed and completed itself. We can most clearly see this mode of development in the activity of our consciousness. In the case of the will, first there is a conception of a goal, and from this, in accordance with circumstances, conceptions appropriate to the realization of the goal are organized systematically. When this organization reaches completion, action begins; through the action, the goal is realized and the activity of the will comes to an end. This holds true not only for the activity of the will but also for thinking, imagination, and other cognitive activities. From the initial conception of a goal emerge various conceptual links; when the appropriate conceptual union is achieved, the cognitive activity has been completed.

As James said in "The Stream of Thought," all consciousness assumes this form. For example, let us suppose a sentence is conceived in consciousness. At the moment that its grammatical subject appears in consciousness, the entire sentence is already implicit. When the predicate appears, the content of the sentence develops and becomes actualized.

This mode is clear in the case of such developed phenomena of consciousness as the will, thinking, and imagination, but in the case of perception and impulse it seems at first glance that the whole is actualized immediately without going through the above process. Regardless of the situation, however, consciousness is never passive or simple but always active and complex, and it is necessarily established through the entire modal process. As voluntarists contend, the will is the original form of consciousness, so all consciousnesses, no matter how simple, are established through the same mode as that of the will.

Impulse and perception differ from volition and thinking in degree, not in kind. A process that is unconscious in the former becomes conscious in the latter. Inferring from this common process, we surmise that the former must have the same structure as the latter. In considering the development of our perception, we find that it arises as the result of

---

1. Nishida here uses the term *jitsuzai* to refer to true reality and the individual realities (entities) in which true reality functions and develops.

various experiences. If we listen to music, for instance, at first no feeling is imparted, but as our ear gradually becomes accustomed to the music, we arrive at a clear perception of it. One can thus assert that perception is a kind of thinking.

We next need to consider misunderstandings caused by the distinction between passive and active consciousness. The aforementioned mode clearly holds for active consciousness, but in passive consciousness, concepts are unified by circumstances in the external world, so it does not appear that a certain total reality develops and completes itself from within. Our consciousness, however, cannot be strictly distinguished as active or passive: this, too, is ultimately a difference of degree. Such activities of consciousness as association and memory are not controlled by a so-called law of association or by other circumstances in the external world. A person's internal qualities are the motivating force behind these activities and a unifying reality develops from within itself. In active consciousness, this unifying reality clearly emerges in consciousness as a conception, while in passive consciousness it is unconscious or functions as a kind of feeling.

The distinction between the active and the passive—the idea that spirit either functions from within or is acted on from without—derives from the assumption that mind and matter exist independently and that phenomena of consciousness arise through the mutual activity of the mind and external objects. This distinction is not found in pure experience, in which the distinction between active and passive is merely a difference of degree. We think of consciousness as active when we have a clear conception of a goal.

According to empiricism, all of our consciousness develops through the activity of external objects. But if there is no internal a priori character to respond to the functions of external things, then no phenomena of consciousness can arise. This is like a seed: no matter how it is nurtured from without, it cannot become a plant unless it has the power of growth within itself. It is also true of course that no plant grows if there is only a seed. Both of these views focus on just one aspect and ignore the other. The activity of true reality is the self-development of a peerless entity;[2] distinctions between the internal and the external and the active and the passive are formulated by thinking in order to explain that development.

I maintain that all phenomena of consciousness are established in the

---

2. The "certain unifying reality" discussed earlier.

same mode. It might seem exceedingly difficult to go a step further and include in that mode the events in the natural world, which are usually deemed phenomena of the external realm, but as I said before, a purely material world apart from consciousness is an abstract concept. True reality is not found outside of phenomena of consciousness, and the true reality realized in direct experience always comes forth in the same mode.

People usually think that fixed material things exist as facts. An actual fact, however, is always an event. As the Greek philosopher Heraclitus said, all things flow and nothing stops.[3] Reality is a succession of events that flow without stopping.

The so-called objective world is not apart from our phenomena of consciousness. Rather, it consists of these phenomena unified by a kind of unifying activity. When the phenomena are universal—when a unity transcendent of the limited, individual consciousness is maintained—we regard them as constituting an independent objective world. For example, a lamp is here before me. If I am the only one who can see it, it might be deemed a subjective hallucination. But when each of us acknowledges it in the same way it becomes an objective fact. The objective, independent world arises from such a universal character.

3. In the original text, Nishida includes a German translation of the original Greek: *Alles fliesst und nichts hat Bestand.*

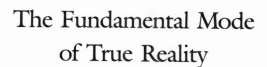

CHAPTER 9

The Fundamental Mode
of True Reality

The facts we experience seem varied, but they are all the same reality and are all established by means of the same mode. Let us now discuss this fundamental mode of reality.

First we must recognize the functioning of a unifying factor behind all of reality. Some scholars think that certain simple, independent constituents—such as the atoms expounded by atomists—are the fundamental reality. Such constituents are abstract concepts formulated for the sake of explanation, and they cannot actually exist. Assume for the sake of argument that here is an atom. It must have some sort of qualities or activity, for that which is without qualities or activity is no different from nothingness. But the functioning of one thing is necessarily in opposition to another, so there must be a third thing to join the first two and enable each to function with respect to the other. For example, when the motion of material object A is transmitted to object B, there must be a force acting between them. And in the case of qualities, when one quality is established, it is established in opposition to another. For instance, if red were the only color, it would not appear to us as such, because for it to do so there must be colors that are not red. Moreover, for one quality to be compared with and distinguished from another, both qualities must be fundamentally identical; two things totally different with no point in common cannot be compared and distinguished. If all things are established through such opposition, then there must be a certain unifying reality concealed at their base.

In the case of material phenomena, this unifying reality is a physical power in the external world; in the case of mental phenomena, it is the unifying power of consciousness. As I stated before, since material phenomena and mental phenomena are identical in pure experience, these two types of unifying activity are fundamentally one: the unifying power at the base of our thinking and willing and the unifying power at the base of the phenomena of the universe are one and the same. The laws of logic and mathematics, for example, are the fundamental principles by which the phenomena of the universe come into being.

In the establishment of reality, then, both a unity at the base of reality and mutual opposition or contradiction are necessary. Heraclitus said that strife is the father of all things—reality is established by contradictions. Red things come into being in opposition to things that are not red, and things that function are established in opposition to things that function reciprocally. When these contradictions disappear, reality disappears as well. On a fundamental level, contradiction and unity are simply two views of one and the same thing. Because there is unity there is contradiction, and because there is contradiction there is unity.[1] Like black and white, things that are the same in all respects except one are the most opposed; but things that have no clear opposition, such as virtue and a triangle, also lack clear unity. The most powerful reality is the one that most thoroughly harmonizes and unifies various contradictions.

The idea that the unifier and the unified are two separate things de-

---

1. In this chapter Nishida begins to articulate the idea of pure experience in a direction that leads eventually to his notion of "absolutely contradictory self-identity."

rives from abstract thinking—in concrete reality the two cannot be separated. A "tree" exists through the unification of the branches, leaves, roots, and trunk, parts that perform various functions. Yet a tree is not merely a collection of these parts, for without a power unifying the entire tree, the various parts are insignificant. A tree exists, then, upon the opposition and unity of its parts.

When the unifying power and that which is unified are split apart, the entity does not become a reality. For example, when a person piles stones, the stones and the person are separate things; the pile of stones is artificial and does not become an independent reality.

The fundamental mode of reality is such that reality is one while it is many and many while it is one; in the midst of equality it maintains distinctions, and in the midst of distinctions it maintains equality.[2] Since these two dimensions cannot be separated, we can say that reality is the self-development of a single entity. Independent, self-sufficient true reality always exhibits this mode; things that do not exhibit this mode are abstract concepts formulated by us.

A reality is that which constitutes in itself a single system. This systematic character induces us to believe that it is an indisputable reality. In contrast, things that do not constitute a system—such as dreams—are believed to be unreal.

A reality that is both one and many must be self-moved and unceasing. A state of quiescence is a state of independent existence free from conflict with others; it is a state of a oneness that rejects plurality. In such a situation, reality cannot come into being.

When a certain state of affairs is established through unity, an opposing state of affairs is necessarily established at the same time. If a unity comes into being a disunity immediately arises and breaks it up. True reality emerges through such infinite opposition. Physicists, basing their argument on the law of the conservation of energy, talk as if there were a limit to reality, but their view is an assumption made for the sake of explanation. Like assertions about a possible limit to space, their view entails abstract consideration of one side of the matter and forgetfulness of the other.

A living thing contains unlimited oppositions and has the ability to give rise to unlimited variation. Spirit is called a living thing because it

---

2. Nishida here echoes the Mahayana Buddhist notion that "distinctions just as they are are equality, and equality just as it is is distinctions."

always includes infinite oppositions and never stops. When it is fixed in a single state and cannot switch to opposing states, it dies.

I have stated that reality is established by means of that which opposes it, but opposition here does not come from other things: it comes from within reality itself. Because there is a unity at the base of opposition, and because unlimited oppositions inevitably develop from the internal character of reality, true reality is the free development that emerges from the internal necessity of a single unifying factor. For example, various geometric forms are possible by virtue of spatial determinations, and while mutually opposing each other they maintain their particular characters. But they do not oppose each other separately, for they are linked by the necessary character of the single factor called space; geometric forms are the unlimited development of spatial qualities. In the same way, what we term natural phenomena do not consist apart from our phenomena of consciousness. They are established by one unifying activity, so they should be regarded as the development of nature as a single entity.

Hegel asserted that any rational thing is real and reality is necessarily rational.[3] Although many thinkers have taken issue with his assertion, people with certain perspectives take it to be an irrefutable truth. No matter how minute, the phenomena of the universe do not occur accidentally with no relation to what precedes or follows them: they necessarily occur for a reason. Our viewing their occurrence as accidental comes from a lack of knowledge.

We usually hold that there is some agent of activity from which activity arises, but in terms of direct experience it is the activity that is real. A so-called agent is an abstract concept, and the idea that there is an agent of activity apart from the activity itself comes from thinking that the opposition between the unity and its content indicates two independent realities.

3. Things are actual as opposed to real (that is, merely existing) to the degree that they embody rationality as a moment in the self-objectification of *Geist* as it goes from being in-itself, to being for-itself (in history), and then to being in-and-for-itself (in human spirit).

CHAPTER 10

The Sole Reality

As I stated before, reality is the activity of consciousness. According to the usual view, the activity of consciousness appears at particular times and then suddenly disappears, making it impossible for one and the same activity of consciousness to be eternally linked together. Does not this perspective lead us to the conclusion that such facts as our life experiences and, on a large scale, the development of the universe up to present, are ultimately things that are in utter confusion without any sort of unifying base, as in the case of empty hallucinations and dreams? I contend that reality comes into being through interrelationship and that the universe is the sole activity of the sole reality.[1]

1. The Japanese term rendered here and in the chapter title as "sole" is *yui-itsu,* which has such other connotations as "unique," "peerless," and "one of a kind."

I have outlined the activity of consciousness as established within a certain sphere by virtue of a unity. Yet many people do not believe that such a unity exists outside that particular sphere—for instance, some think that yesterday's and today's consciousnesses are totally independent and cannot be regarded as one consciousness. From the standpoint of direct experience, however, this distinction is relative, not ultimate. And in the case of thinking and the will, which all people think of as unified phenomena of consciousness, the process involved is nothing more than a succession of different ideas. If we draw fine distinctions between the successive ideas, we can think of them as separate consciousnesses; but if we view them not as separate, individual realities but as one activity of consciousness, then we can regard yesterday's and today's consciousnesses as a single activity of consciousness. When we consider a problem or plan an enterprise over several days, one and the same consciousness is functioning over time, though for different durations on each full appearance.

The union of consciousness includes a simultaneous union as in perception, a continuous union as in association and thinking, and a union that spans one's lifetime as in self-awareness. These unions differ in degree, but they all exhibit the same character of consciousness. Some thinkers maintain that phenomena of consciousness change from moment to moment, that the same consciousness does not occur twice, and that yesterday's and today's consciousnesses are totally different even when they have the same content. These thinkers do not view consciousness from the standpoint of direct experience; rather, they presuppose time and infer that phenomena of consciousness are things that appear in time. If phenomena of consciousness are established through the form of time, then because of the unidirectional nature of time, phenomena of consciousness that have passed cannot return. Even if they are consciousnesses with exactly the same content, the form of time is such that they are not identical. But if we return to the base of direct experience, we see that the relationship between consciousness and time is the reverse. Because time is nothing more than a form that orders the content of our experience, the content of consciousness must first be able to be joined, be united, and become one in order for the idea of time to arise. Otherwise we would not be able to link things sequentially and thereby think in terms of time. The unifying activity of consciousness is not controlled by time; on the contrary, time is established by the unifying activity. At the base of consciousness there is a transcendent, unchanging reality apart from time.

From the perspective of direct experience, consciousnesses with the same content are the same consciousness. In the same way that truth is the same regardless of when and by whom it is thought, our consciousness yesterday and our consciousness today belong to the same system and have the same content, so they are directly joined and become a single consciousness. The life of an individual is the development of consciousness that constitutes such a single system.

There is always a certain unchanging reality at the base of the mind. This reality enlarges the development of consciousness from day to day. The passage of time is the continuous change of the unifying center that accompanies this development, and this center is always "the present."

Granted that an unchanging, unifying power functions at the base of consciousness, one might wonder about its form and how it maintains itself. Psychology reduces the origin of this unifying activity to the material called the brain. As we saw before, however, the supposition of an independent material body apart from consciousness is an inference from the unchanging union of phenomena of consciousness, so it is really the unifying activity behind the union of the content of consciousness, and not the material body, that is the fundamental fact. This unifying power does not emerge from another reality; rather, reality is established by its activity. All people believe that there is a fixed, unchanging principle in the universe and that all things are established according to it. This principle is the power that unifies consciousness; it is not possessed by mind or matter but establishes them. It is independent and self-sustaining, and it does not vary according to time, space, or the person—it does not change under any circumstances.

"Principle" might be thought of as referring to the activity that controls the linkage of ideas in our subjective consciousness. But this activity is the trace of that principle's functioning, not the principle itself. The principle is creative, and although we can become it and function in accordance with it, we cannot see it as an object of consciousness.

To say that something exists in the ordinary sense means that it exists in a certain form in a certain time and place. But the existence denoted by the principle of which I speak is different. If it were restricted to one place, it could not perform its unifying function and would fall short of being a living, true principle.

In the the same way that an individual's consciousness constitutes a single reality in which yesterday's and today's consciousnesses are united, consciousness that spans a lifetime can likewise be regarded as singular. Taking this farther, we see that this is not limited to the scope of just one individual, for a person can likewise link his or her own consciousness with that of another and regard them as a single consciousness. Just as a principle is the same no matter who thinks about it, at the base of our consciousness there is something universal. By means of it we are able to communicate with and understand one another. Universal reason runs throughout the base of our minds, and no matter how endowed with originality, each person born in a particular society is swayed by the particular social spirit. Expressed metaphorically, each person's spirit is simply one cell of the social spirit.

As I said before, the union of the consciousnesses of two people and the union of yesterday's and today's consciousnesses in one person are the same. The former pair seem to be joined indirectly from without and the latter directly from within. Viewing both pairs as joined from without, we can argue that the person's present and past consciousnesses are joined by signs in a type of internal sensation, just as consciousnesses between individuals are joined together by linguistic and other signs. Viewing both pairs as joined from within, we can argue that consciousnesses between individuals are joined directly because of a single common foundation.

As I have stated several times before, the so-called objective world does not come into existence apart from our subjectivity, for the unifying power of the objective world and that of subjective consciousness are identical; the objective world and consciousness are established according to the same principle. For this reason we can understand the fundamental principle constitutive of the universe by means of the principle within the self. If the world were something different from the unity of our consciousness, we could never make contact with it. The world we can know and understand is established by a unifying power identical to that of our consciousness.

CHAPTER II

The Development
of Reality
through Differentiation

From the perspective that the world exists apart from consciousness, we might say that all things exist individually and independently, but from the standpoint that phenomena of consciousness are the sole reality, we must say that there is one unifying power at the base of the myriad things in the universe and that these things are the developmental expression of one and the same reality. As our knowledge advances, we come to greater and greater certainty that there is such a single principle. I now will discuss how this sole reality gives rise to various discriminative oppositions.

At the same time that reality is a unified whole, it must include opposition. If there is a real entity here, then there is necessarily another that opposes it. In such mutual opposition, the two entities are not totally independent realities, for they must be unified; they must be part of the development of one reality through differentiation. When they are unified and emerge as one reality, another opposition then emerges. At the same time, another unity must also be functioning behind this further opposition. In this way reality develops into an unlimited unity. From the opposite angle, we can say that an unlimited, single reality develops itself through differentiation from the small to the large, from the shallow to the deep. This process is the mode of the manifestation of reality, and the phenomena of the universe come into being and advance in accordance with it.

This developmental process of reality can be seen clearly in phenomena of consciousness. For example, the will attempts to realize certain ideals, and in this way it entails a conflict between the actual and the ideal. When the will is put into practice and realizes the ideal, other ideals come to stand in opposition to this newly realized actuality and a new will then emerges. We continue to develop and to actualize ourselves in this way throughout our lives. We also discover this mode of reality in the daily life and development of living things in general, for they exhibit such unceasing activity. Though it might seem a bit difficult to conceive of the existence of nonliving things in terms of this mode, I will consider that later in my discussion of nature.

How is it that various differentiations of reality emerge along the lines of the aforementioned fundamental mode of reality? First, we must consider the origin of the distinction between subject and object. Subject and object do not exist separately, for they are the two relative sides of one reality. Our subjectivity is the unifying aspect, whereas objectivity is the unified aspect; the self is always the entity that unifies reality, whereas things are the entities that are unified. "Objectivity" does not here signify a reality independent of our consciousness; it is simply the phenomena of consciousness.) For example, when we perceive or think about something, the self is the activity that compares and unifies this and that. So-called things are objects standing over and against the self; they are the material of comparison and unification. When we view an earlier consciousness from a later one, we might think that we can see the self as an object, but the self we see is not the true self, for the true self is the present observer or unifier. At this time, the earlier unity has already been completed and is included in the next one as its material. The self is an infinite unifier and can never be made the object of comparison and unification.

Even psychology construes the self as the unifier of consciousness. Seen from the perspective that consciousness is the sole true reality, the self is the unifier of reality. Although the self as unifier is regarded in psychology as separate from that which is unified, such a self is simply an abstract concept. In fact, there is no self apart from things—our self is the very unifier of the universe.

The distinction between mental and material phenomena in no way signifies that there are two kinds of reality. Mental phenomena are the unifying aspect, the subjective side, whereas material phenomena are that which is unified, the objective side. In the distinction between the two, a single reality is viewed from two opposite sides. In the aspect of the unity, then, all things belong to subjectivity and are mental phenomena; setting aside that unity, we see all things as objective, material phenomena. (The conflict between idealism and materialism stems from their respective attachment to only one of these two sides.)

Next, from what does the distinction between active and passive derive? There is no distinction between active and passive in reality, for they are the two sides of one reality; the unifier is always active and the unified is always passive. In the case of phenomena of consciousness, for example, to say that our will has functioned means that the will's unifying idea—namely, a goal—has been realized and that a unity has been established. To say that the mind has functioned means that the goal of unity has been attained; when this is not possible and the mind has been unified by another, the situation is said to be passive. In material phenomena as well, to say that entity A functions in opposition to entity B means that the qualities of A have been able to include and control the qualities of B. In this sense, unity is what "active" truly means, and when we are in a position of unity, we are active and free. In contrast, when we are unified by another, we are passive and controlled by the law of necessity.

Usually, that which comes first in a temporal progression is thought of as an active entity, but this is not necessarily the case. An active entity must have power. By power I mean the unifying activity of reality. For example, the movement of physical bodies is said to come from kinetic energy. But since power indicates a certain unchanging relationship between phenomena, it refers to the unifier that joins and integrates them. Strictly speaking, only spirit is active.

We next need to examine the distinction between the unconscious and consciousness. The aforementioned subjective unifying activity is always unconscious, and the object of that unification comes forth as the content of consciousness. In both thinking and willing, the true unifying activity is always unconscious. Only when we reflect on it does it appear in consciousness as a conception; at this time it is no longer a unifying activity, but the object of unification. As I said before, because the unifying activity is always subjective, it must always be unconscious. Hartmann[1] has claimed that the unconscious is an activity; in like manner, when we stand in the position of subjectivity in a state of activity, the unifying activity is always unconscious. In contrast, when we become conscious of a certain consciousness as an objective entity, that consciousness has already lost its activity. For example, while training in a certain art, as long as we are conscious of every movement we have yet to embody a truly living art, but when we arrive at a state of unconsciousness, the art comes alive in us for the first time.

From the standpoint of psychology, all mental phenomena are phenomena of consciousness, so we might make the criticism that unconscious mental phenomena do not exist. But our mental phenomena are not merely a series of ideas—there is, of necessity, an unconscious activity that links and unites them, and only then do they come into being.

Finally, we can explain the relation between *phenomenon* and *noumenon* as the relation between two aspects of reality. Noumenon refers to the unifying power of reality, whereas phenomenon indicates the state of conflict in reality's development through differentiation. To say, for example, that the noumenon of this desk exists means that our consciousness appears repeatedly by means of a set union, and the unchanging noumenon here indicates the unifying power of this reality.

We must further argue that true subjectivity is the fundamental nature—the noumenon—of reality. Though we usually think that material things are to be found in objectivity, this thought derives from consideration of abstract subjectivity rather than true subjectivity. Such an abstract subjectivity is a powerless concept, and relative to it the noumenon

---

1. Eduard von Hartmann (1842–1906), a German philosopher, focused on the relationship between the unconscious and consciousness in such works as *Philosophy of the Unconscious* and *Phenomenology of the Moral Consciousness*.

of a thing belongs to objectivity. But the truth is that an object apart from the subject is also a powerless, abstract concept. The noumenon of a truly active thing must be the unifying power that is the fundamental activity in the establishment of reality—that is, it must be true subjectivity.

CHAPTER 12

Nature

Although there is only one reality, it appears in various forms in accordance with differing views of it. Nature conceived of as an objective reality totally independent of our subjectivity is an abstract concept, not true reality. The noumenal aspect of nature is the fact of direct experience in which subject and object have not yet separated. For example, what we regard as true grass and trees are grass and trees with living color and forms—they are intuitive facts. Only when we separate the subjective activity from the concrete reality can we think of the grass and trees as purely objective nature. By taking this way of thinking to the extreme, we arrive of the idea of nature in the strictest sense as construed by scientists. This idea is the most abstract and most removed from the true state of reality.

What people usually refer to as *nature* is what remains after the subjective aspect, the unifying activity, is removed from concrete reality. For this reason, there is no self in nature. Nature is simply moved from without according to the law of necessity, and it cannot function spontaneously from within. The linkage and union of natural phenomena is not an internal unity as in mental phenomena, but an accidental linkage in time and space. The laws of nature, attained through the law of induction, are simply assumptions that because two types of phenomena arise in an unchanging succession, one is the cause of the other. No matter how far the natural sciences develop, we obtain no deeper explanation than this one, which becomes ever more detailed and encompassing.

The present tendency of science is to strive to become as objective as possible. As a result, psychological phenomena are explained physiologically, physiological phenomena chemically, chemical phenomena physically, and physical phenomena mechanically. What is the nature of the purely mechanical perspective at the foundation of this type of explanation? Pure matter is a reality we cannot even begin to experience, but assuming for the sake of argument that we can experience it to some extent, it must be something that comes forth in our consciousness as a phenomenon of consciousness. Yet all things that appear as facts of consciousness are subjective and cannot be deemed purely objective matter. Moreover, pure matter has no positive qualities that we can grasp; it possesses only purely quantitative characteristics such as spatial and temporal movement. Like a mathematical concept, it is nothing more than a completely abstract concept.

Matter is thought of as something that fills space and can be directly perceived, but the extension of things of which we can think concretely is simply a conscious phenomenon of touch and sight. Even though things may seem large in our sensation of them, they do not necessarily consist of a large amount of matter. Because the amount of physical matter is determined in physics by the amount of energy present,—that is, it is inferred from functional relationships between physical things— it is never an intuitive fact.

Moreover, if we think of nature in the purely material terms discussed above, then there are no distinctions between animals, plants, and life in general, and there is nothing except the activity of a mechanical energy that is everywhere the same. In this approach, natural phenomena lose all of their special characteristics and significance; human beings are no different from clods of dirt.

The real nature that we actually experience is never an abstract concept as described above; nor is it merely an activity of a uniform mechanical energy. Animals are animals, plants are plants, and metals are metals; each is a concrete fact with its own special characteristics and significance. The things that we designate as mountains, rivers, grasses, trees, insects, fish, birds, and beasts all have their own respective individuality. We can explain them from a variety of standpoints and in a variety of ways, but nature in the sense of directly given, intuitive facts cannot be altered in the least.

We usually take purely mechanical nature to be the truly objective reality and concrete nature in direct experience to be a subjective phenomenon, but these ideas are inferred from the assumption that all phenomena of consciousness are subjective phenomena of the self. And as I have said, we can in no way posit a reality apart from the phenomena of consciousness. If we say that something is subjective because it is related to phenomena of consciousness, then purely mechanical nature is subjective as well, for we cannot think of such things as time, space, and motion apart from our phenomena of consciousness. They are only relatively—not absolutely—objective.

Nature as a truly concrete reality does not come into being without having a unifying activity. Nature therefore possesses a kind of self, too. The various forms, variations, and motions a plant or animal expresses are not mere unions or mechanical movements of insignificant matter; because each has an inseparable relationship to the whole, each should be regarded as a developmental expression of one unifying self. For example, the paws, legs, nose, mouth, and other parts of an animal all have a close relation to the goal of survival, and we cannot understand their significance if we consider them apart from this fact. In explaining the phenomena of plants and animals, we must posit the unifying power of nature. Biologists explain all the phenomena of living things in terms of life instincts. This unifying activity is found not only in living things, but is present to some extent even in inorganic crystals, and all minerals have a particular crystalline form. The self of nature, that is, its unifying activity, becomes clearer as we move from inorganic crystals to organisms like plants and animals (with the true self first appearing in spirit).

From the standpoint of the strictly mechanical explanation of present-day science, the teleological development of organisms must be explained in terms of the laws of physics and chemistry. This development comes to be viewed as a mere accidental outcome. Because this view largely disregards facts, scientists try to explain this development through the assumption of a potential power. They say that eggs or seeds possess a potential power that gives rise to the respective organisms. This potential power corresponds to the unifying power of nature we have been discussing.

Even if in our explanation of nature we allow for the activity of such a unifying power apart from mechanical energy, the two need not clash but can complement each other to achieve a complete explanation of nature. Let us take, for example, a bronze statue. The bronze, the statue's raw material, obeys physical and chemical laws yet we cannot view the statue as a mere lump of bronze, for it is a work of art that expresses our ideals. It appeared by means of the unifying power of our ideals. The unifying activity of the ideals and the physical and chemical laws that control the raw material belong to different spheres, and in no way do they clash with each other.

Only when there is a unifying self does nature have a goal, take on significance, and become a truly living nature. The unifying power that is the life of such nature is not an abstract concept artificially created by our thought but a fact that appears in our intuition. When we see our favorite flower or pet animal, we immediately grasp a certain unifying reality in the whole. This reality is the thing's self, its fundamental nature or noumenon. Artists are people who most excel in this kind of intuition. They discern at a glance the truth of a thing and grasp its unifying reality. What they then express is not a superficial fact but an unchanging noumenal reality hidden deep within things.

Goethe devoted himself to the study of living things[1] and pioneered the present-day theory of evolution. According to his theory, there is behind natural phenomena an "original" phenomenon (*Urphänomen*), which is intuited by poets. Further, the various plants and animals in our world are variations of the original plant and original animal, and present-day plants and animals all reflect a fixed, unchanging pattern. Based on this theory, Goethe argues that all living things have evolved.

---

1. Goethe pursued research in botany (*Die Metamorphose der Pflanzen*, 1790). His scientific bent also led him to produce a work on optics (*Zur Farbenlehre*, 1810).

But what sort of thing is the unifying self behind nature? Because we think of natural phenomena as purely objective phenomena unrelated to our subjectivity, the unifying power of nature is thought to be unknowable. In true reality, however, subjectivity and objectivity are not separate, and actual nature is not a purely objective, abstract concept but a concrete fact of consciousness that includes both subject and object. Accordingly, the unifying self behind nature is not some unknowable entity totally unrelated to our consciousness but actually none other than the unifying activity of consciousness. Our understanding of the significance and *telos* of nature is thus made possible by virtue of the subjective unification of the self 's ideals, feeling, and volition. For example, our ability to understand the fundamental significance of various organs and behaviors of animals comes from our intuiting it directly through our feeling and will—if we did not have feeling and will we could not even begin to understand it. As our ideals, feeling, and volition gain greater depth and width, we become increasingly able to understand the true significance of nature. Our subjective unity and the objective unifying power of nature are originally identical. If we view this objectively, it is the unifying power of nature, and if we view it subjectively, it is the unity of self 's knowledge, feeling, and volition.

Some people believe that material force is completely unrelated to our subjective unity. Although it may be the most insignificant unity, even this force does not exist apart from subjective unity. Our belief that there is a force in matter that performs various functions comes from viewing the self 's volitional activity objectively.

People usually think that the inference of nature's significance through the self 's ideals, feeling, or volition is simply an analogical inference and hence not a firm truth. But their view originates in thinking of subjectivity and objectivity independently and regarding mind and nature as two different types of reality. From the perspective of pure experience, we view them as identical.

CHAPTER 13

Spirit

At a glance, nature appears to be a purely objective reality independent of spirit,[1] but actually, it is not separate from subjectivity. Seen in terms of their subjective aspect, that is, the unifying activity, so-called natural phenomena are all phenomena of consciousness. For example, here is a stone; if we assume that it has come into being through the power of a certain unknowable reality independent of our subjectivity, then it becomes nature. If we directly view the stone as a fact of direct experience,

---

1. The Japanese term *seishin*, rendered here as "spirit," is roughly equivalent to the German term *Geist* and therefore might also be rendered "mind" or "psyche." Due to the religious connotations of *seishin* found later in this work, we have translated it as "spirit."

however, it is not an objectively independent reality but a union of our senses of sight, touch, and so forth; it is a phenomenon of consciousness, established by the unity of our consciousness. When we return to the base of direct experience and view so-called natural phenomena, we grasp them as phenomena of consciousness that are established by subjective unity. This viewpoint generates the idealist statement that the world is our ideas.

Some people believe that when we see the same stone, each of us has the same idea of it. Actually, though, our ideas differ according to our character and experiences. Concrete reality is therefore entirely subjective and individual, and so-called objective reality disappears, for it is simply an abstract concept that we all share.

What then is that which we usually call spirit in opposition to nature? What kind of thing is a subjective phenomenon of consciousness? So-called mental phenomena are simply the unifying or active aspect of reality considered abstractly. In reality as it truly exists there are no distinctions between subjectivity and objectivity or spirit and matter, and in the establishment of reality, a unifying activity is necessary. This unifying activity is not apart from reality, though when we view it abstractly and think of it as something standing in opposition to unified objects, it is seen as a mental phenomenon. For example, we might have a sensation here and now, but it is not independent of all other things—it is established in opposition to something else, that is, in comparison with and distinguished from another. This activity of comparison and distinction—the unifying activity—is what we call spirit. As this activity develops, the distinction between spirit and matter becomes increasingly clear. In childhood, our spirit is natural, and the activity of subjectivity is therefore weak. As we mature, the unifying activity flourishes, and we attain to an awareness of our spirit as distinguished from objective nature.

For this reason, people usually consider spirit an independent reality distinguished from objective nature. Yet, just as purely objective nature apart from the subjective unity of spirit is an abstract concept, a purely subjective spirit apart from objective nature is an abstract concept as well. There is something that is unified and an activity that does the unifying. Even though we might assume that there is an essence of spirit that senses the activity of things in the world, there is a thing that functions and a mind that senses it. Spirit that does not function, like things that do not function, is unknowable.

But for what reason is the unifying activity of reality distinguished from its content (that which can be unified), and why does it emerge as if it were an independent reality? The answer undoubtedly lies in the contradictions and conflicts of the various unities in reality. There are various systems—various unities—in reality; when these systematic unities conflict with and contradict each other, they appear clearly in consciousness. Where there are conflicts and contradictions there is spirit, and where there is spirit there are conflicts and contradictions. In the case of volitional action, for example, when there are no conflicts between motives, there is no consciousness, and this approaches so-called objective nature. As the conflict between motives becomes more distinct, one can become clearly conscious of the will and aware of one's mind.[2]

From where do the conflicts and contradictions of a system arise? They arise from the character of reality itself. As I said before, while reality is infinite conflict, it is also infinite unity. Conflict is an indispensable aspect of unity, for it is through conflict that we advance to an even greater unity. Our spirit, the unifying activity of reality, is conscious of itself not when that unity is functioning, but when there is conflict.

When we have matured in an art, that is, when we have attained to the unity of reality, we are unconscious and do not know our own unity. As we try to advance to even greater depths, conflicts arise with that which has already been attained, and in this encounter we become conscious again, for consciousness is always born of such conflicts. The fact that conflicts necessarily accompany spirit should be seen in light of the fact that spirit is accompanied by ideals. Ideals signify contradiction and conflict with actuality. (Since our spirit appears through conflict, there is always suffering in spirit, and the claim of pessimists that our world is characterized by suffering contains an element of truth.)

If we see our spirit as the unifying activity of reality, we must say that there is a unity to all things in reality, that there is spirit in it. On what basis do we separate living and non-living things and distinguish that which has spirit from that which does not? Strictly speaking, we can say that there is spirit throughout reality; and as I said before, there is a unifying self in nature as well, a unifying power identical to our spirit. If a tree, for example, as a phenomenon of consciousness were to appear here, we would ordinarily think of it as an objective reality established by natural powers, but if we see it as constituting a system of phenomena

---

2. The Japanese term here used for "mind" *kokoro,* which can also be rendered "heart"— it includes nuances of both "mind" and "heart."

of consciousness, then it is established by the unifying activity of consciousness. In so-called non-living things, the unifying self has not yet appeared in actuality as a fact of direct experience. The tree itself is not aware of the unifying activity of the self; the unifying self is found in another thing's consciousness, not in the tree itself. The tree is merely a thing unified from outside, not something unified internally, and for this reason it is not yet an independent, self-fulfilled reality. In the contrasting case of animals, an internal unity or self is expressing itself in actuality, and we can view all of the various phenomena of animals (such as their form and behavior) as expressions of this internal unity. All of reality is established through unity, and in spirit the unity emerges as a clear fact. It is only in spirit that reality becomes a perfect reality, an independent, self-fulfilled reality.

In things without spirit, the unity is given from without, and hence it is not an internal unity of the self. The unity hence changes in accordance with the viewer. For instance, we might think that there is a single reality called a tree, but in the eyes of a chemist, the tree is an organic compound, a combination of chemical elements. We might therefore say that there is in fact no separate reality called a tree. But we cannot view the spirit of animals in this way. Although we can regard the physical body of an animal, like a plant, as a compound, spirit cannot be changed in accordance with the viewer; no matter what interpretation we offer, it truly expresses an unmoving unity.

Modern evolutionary theory contends that evolution proceeds from inorganic matter to plants, then to animals, and finally to human beings. This theory indicates that reality gradually expresses its hidden essence as actuality. It is only in the development of spirit that the fundamental character of the establishment of reality appears. As Leibniz said, evolution is involution.

Our self, as the unifier of spirit, is the fundamental unifying activity of reality. According to one school of psychology, the self is simply a union of ideas and feelings apart from which there is no self. This view neglects the side of unity and entails consideration of the self from the side of analytical distinctions only. If we look at all things analytically, we cannot find a unifying activity. But we cannot allow the analytical way of viewing things to make us disregard this activity. Things are established by a unity, and ideas and feelings are made into concrete reality through the power of a unifying self. This unifying power called the self is an expression of the unifying power of reality; it is an eternal unchanging power. Our self is therefore felt to be always creative, free, and infinitely active.

As I said before, though we may reflect inwardly and sense a kind of feeling that is somehow the self, this self is not the true self, for it cannot act. Only when the unity of reality functions inwardly do we feel that we control reality according to our own ideals and that the self is engaging in free activity. Because the unifying activity of reality is infinite, we feel our self to be infinite and to envelop the universe.

From the standpoint of pure experience, the unifying activity of reality of which I speak might be thought of as simply an abstract idea rather than as a fact of direct experience. The facts of our direct experience, however, are not ideas or feelings but the activity of the will, and the unifying activity is an indispensable element of direct experience.

Until now I have considered spirit in opposition to nature—henceforth I want to think a bit about the relation between spirit and nature. Our spirit is usually considered to be the unifying function of reality and to be a special reality vis-à-vis nature. But in actuality, there is no unifying activity apart from that which is unified and no subjective spirit apart from objective nature. To say that we know a thing simply means that the self unites with it. When one sees a flower, the self has become the flower. To investigate a flower and elucidate its basic nature means to discard all of the self 's subjective conjectures and thereby unite with the basic nature of the flower. Similarly, reason is not a subjective fancy, for it is not only something common to all people but also the fundamental principle by which objective reality is established. Indisputable truth is gained by constantly discarding our subjective self and becoming objective. To say that our knowledge becomes more profound means that we unite ourselves with objective nature.

This holds not only for knowledge but also for the will. If we are purely subjective, we can do nothing. The will is able to realize itself only by according with objective nature. To move water is to accord with its nature, to control people is to accord with their nature, and to control oneself is to accord with one's own nature. Our wills are effective to the degree that they become objective. Thousands of years after their deaths, Sākyamuni and Christ still have the power to move people only because their spirit was truly objective. Those without a self—those who have extinguished the self—are the greatest.

We usually distinguish mental phenomena and material phenomena in terms of internal and external, thinking of the former as internal and the latter as external. This view originates in the arbitrary assumption that spirit is within the body. But when seen from the perspective of direct experience, all things are phenomena of consciousness, without distinction between internal and external. That which we speak of as the internal, subjective spirit is a highly superficial and feeble spirit, an individual fancy. In contrast, great, deep spirit is the activity of the universe that is united with the truth of the universe. Such spirit of itself accompanies the activity of the external world, and it does nothing but act. The inspiration of an artist is an example of this.

In closing this chapter, I want to say a word about the joy and suffering of the human mind. When our spirit is in a state of completion, a state of unity, we experience pleasure, and when it is in an incomplete state, a state of disunion, we experience pain. As I said, spirit is the unifying activity of reality, and contradictions and conflicts necessarily accompany this unity. We always experience pain when these contradictions and conflicts occur, and the infinite unifying activity immediately attempts to rid itself of them and to achieve an even greater unity. In this attempt, various desires and ideals arise in us, and when we attain to the greater unity—when we are able to satisfy our desires and ideals— we experience pleasure. Thus, one facet of pleasure necessarily includes pain, and one facet of pain is necessarily accompanied by pleasure. This being the case, the human mind cannot arrive at absolute pleasure, but it can maintain infinite happiness when, by effort, it becomes objective and unites with nature.

Psychologists say that what assists our living is pleasure, and what hinders it is pain. Because life is the development of the basic nature of living things—that is, the maintenance of the unity of the self—this theory is the same as saying that whatever supports unity is pleasure and that whatever hinders it is pain.

Again, spirit is the unifying activity of reality. Because great spirit unites with nature, when we take our small self as our self we experience much pain; when the self becomes larger and unites with objective nature, we experience happiness.

CHAPTER 14

God as Reality

I have argued that nature and spirit are not two completely different kinds of reality. The distinction between them results from differing ways of looking at one and the same reality. Anyone who deeply comprehends nature discerns a spiritual unity at its base. Moreover, complete, true spirit is united with nature; only one reality exists in the universe. And, as I said before, this sole reality is both infinite opposition and conflict and infinite unity. It is an independent, self-fulfilled, infinite activity. We call the base of this infinite activity God. God is not something that transcends reality, God is the base of reality. God is that which dissolves the distinction between subjectivity and objectivity and unites spirit and nature.

Regardless of the historical age or the cultural group, everyone has a word for "God." Due to differences in the level of knowledge and the diversity of demands, the word is interpreted in a variety of ways. Most people of religion conceive of God as something like a great human who stands outside the universe and controls it. This notion of God is extremely infantile, and it not only conflicts with present-day learning and knowledge but in the religious sphere falls short of being something with which we humans can achieve intimate unity in our hearts. At the same time, however, I cannot follow the lead of hard-core scientists these days and argue that matter is the only reality and that material force is the basis of the universe. As previously stated, there is a fundamental spiritual principle at the base of reality, and this principle is God. This idea accords with the fundamental truth of Indian religion: Ātman and Brahman are identical. God is the great spirit of the universe.

Since long ago, there have been many attempts to prove the existence of God. Some people argue that because this world could not have begun from nothing it must have been created by something, namely, God. Thus relying on the law of causality, such people consider God to be the cause of the world. Others hold that this world does not exist by accident, that it is in all respects something with meaning, organized with a certain fixed goal; they then infer that something gave this organization to the world and conclude by claiming that the organizing guide is God. They view the relation between the world and God like that between an artistic work and the artist. Both of these arguments attempt to prove the existence of God from the standpoint of knowledge and to determine God's qualities. There are others who try to prove God's existence by referring to moral demands totally divorced from knowledge. They argue that humans have moral demands, that is, consciences, and that if there were no great supervisor in the world to encourage good and admonish evil, then our morality would be meaningless. It is for this reason, they say, that we must acknowledge the existence of God as the upholder of morality. Kant is one who advanced this proof.

But can these arguments really prove the existence of God? Although some contend that because there has to be a cause of the world we must acknowledge the existence of God, if we base our argument on the law of causality can we not proceed another step and ask about the cause of God? And if we were to say that God is beginningless and endless and hence exists without a cause, is there any reason why we cannot say the same thing about the world? Also, to infer an omniscient controller from the fact that the world is organized favorably according to a certain goal, one must prove that the myriad things in the universe are in fact created purposefully, but this is extremely difficult to do. If the proof of God's existence hinges on this, then the existence of God becomes quite uncertain. Some might believe it, while others might not. Even supposing that this fact is proven, we can still think of the world as coming into being by chance and yet having a goal.

The attempt to prove the existence of God from moral demands is even weaker. If there is an omniscient, omnipotent God who upholds our morality, we do gain great strength in the moral realm; but though the belief that God exists has a valuable impact on our behavior, it does not prove that God does indeed exist. We can even view this belief as simply an expediency.

The aforementioned theories attempt to prove the existence of God indirectly from without and thus have not proven God immediately in the direct experience of the self. How can we verify the existence of God in facts of our direct experience? An infinite power is hidden even in our small chests that are restricted by time and space; the infinite unifying power of reality is latent in us. Possessing this power, we can search for the truth of the universe in learning, we can express the true meaning of reality in art, and we can know the foundation of reality that forms the universe in the depths of our hearts—we can grasp the true face of God. The infinitely free activity of the human heart proves God directly. As Jakob Boehme said, we see God with a "reversed eye" (*umgewandtes Auge*).[1]

If we seek God in the facts of the external world, God must inescapably be a hypothetical God. Further, a God set up outside the universe as a creator or overseer of the universe cannot be deemed a true, absolutely infinite God. The religion of India of the distant past and the mysticism that flourished in Europe in the fifteenth and sixteenth centuries sought God in intuition realized in the inner soul, and this I consider to be the deepest knowledge of God.

In what form does God exist? From one perspective, taken by such thinkers as Nicholas of Cusa, God is all negation, whereas that which can be affirmed or grasped is not God; if there is some entity that can

---

1. Jakob Boehme (1575–1624), a German mystic and philosopher, had numerous mystical experiences, on the basis of which he described God as an *Ungrund*—a bottomless abyss from which the Trinity and the universe emerge.

be grasped, it is already finite and cannot perform the infinite activity of unifying the universe.[2] From this standpoint, God is absolute nothingness. God is not, however, mere nothingness. An immovable unifying activity clearly functions at the base of the establishment of reality, and it is by means of this activity that reality is established. For example, where is the law that the sum of the three angles in a triangle is equal to the sum of two right angles? We can neither see nor hear this law, yet does there not exist an indisputable law? Further, in response to a great painting, we see that something in its entirety strikes sensitive people as enlivened by a superb spirit; but if we try to determine how each object or scene in the painting is enlivened by this spirit, we inevitably fail. God is in these senses the unifier of the universe, the base of reality; and because God is no-thing, there is no place where God is not, and no place where God does not function.

In the same way that profound mathematics gives no knowledge to those who cannot understand mathematical principles and that a sublime painting does not move those who have no feel for beauty, the existence of God is considered a fancy or felt to be meaningless and therefore ignored by mediocre and shallow humans. Those who desire to know the true God must discipline themselves and provide themselves with eyes that can know God. To such people, the power of God is active in the universe just as a painter's spirit is active in a great painting; God's power is felt as a fact of direct experience. This is the fact of seeing God.

Given what I have said so far, God might be felt to be a cold philosophical existence—the base of the unity of the universe—totally unrelated to the activity of our warm feelings, but this is hardly the case. As stated, since our desires arise in the search for a greater unity, we experience joy when we attain to this unity. The so-called self-love of an individual is ultimately nothing more than this demand for unity. Because our infinite spirit is never fundamentally satisfied by the unity constituted by an individual self, it inevitably seeks a larger unity, a great self that envelops both oneself and others. We come to express sympathy toward others and seek congruence and unity between oneself and others. Our

2. Nishida's note is "Nicholas Cusanus, *De docta ignorantia,* cap.24." Nicholas of Cusa (1401–1464) is known for his articulation of the *via negativa,* the mystical way of negation, especially in terms of "learned ignorance" and the unity of opposites (*coincidentia oppositorum*).

love for others is the demand for such a supra-individual unity with them. Accordingly, we feel greater peace and joy in love for others than in love for ourselves. God, the unity of the universe, is the base of this unifying activity, the foundation of our love, the source of our joy. God is infinite love, infinite joy, and peace.

PART III

The Good

CHAPTER 15

Conduct (1)

I have discussed reality in outline, and I will now consider such practical issues as what we ought to do, what the good is, and what the basis of human action ought to be. I believe we can subsume the various phenomena of the practical human realm within the category of conduct, so I will first examine the nature of conduct.

Seen from the outside, conduct is the movement of the body. It differs from such physical movements as the flow of water or the falling of a stone in that it is goal-oriented and possesses a kind of consciousness. Conduct must be distinguished from the following two kinds of movements: organisms' reflex movements that are goal-oriented but unconscious; and as seen in relatively higher animals, instinctive action that is goal-oriented and involves some consciousness, but in which the goals are not clearly known. Conduct is physical action in which the goal is clearly known in consciousness. Having bodies, humans make a variety of physical movements, including reflexive and instinctual actions, but that which can be rightly called the activity of the self is limited to conduct in the above sense.

Conduct is often accompanied by movement in the external world—that is, by physical actions—but because the element critical to conduct is the presence of a phenomenon of consciousness in the internal world, let us consider from a psychological point of view the kind of consciousness that is involved in conduct. As we saw before, conduct is physical action that arises because of a conscious goal; it is willed action. When we speak of conduct, the term includes action in the external world, but when we speak of the will, it mainly indicates internal phenomena of consciousness. Therefore to discuss the phenomena of consciousness that is involved in conduct is to discuss the will.

How does the will arise? The human body is fundamentally constructed so as to make movements appropriate for preserving and developing its own life. Consciousness, arising together with these movements, is initially the simple feeling of pain or pleasure. But as ideas regarding the external world gradually become clearer and the activity of association becomes active, the initial movements no longer occur unconsciously in response to stimuli from the external world; rather, one first generates an idea of a result, then generates an idea of the movements that can serve as the means to the result, and finally shifts to actual movement. In this way, the will arises.

For the will to arise, then, there must be a physical or mental cause that initially determines the direction of movement or, in terms of consciousness, the direction of association. This cause appears in consciousness as a kind of impulsive feeling. Without asking whether it is innate or learned, we should simply call it the power of the will. Here, however, I shall call it motivation.

Motivation must be accompanied by an idea of a result, by a goal or, more precisely, by an idea of a goal. This idea is acquired through experience and elicited by association. Because the form of the will is established at this time, I call this idea a desire, and it is the first stage of the will. When there is only one desire, it generates actions in conjunction with an idea of movement; when there are two or more desires, a conflict of desires occurs and it is the most powerful desire, occupying the principal position in consciousness, that generates actions. I call this decision. The will is the entirety of these phenomena of consciousness. At times it indicates, in a narrow sense, the activity at the moment of the shift to action or, in particular, to decision.

The will as an internal phenomenon of consciousness, not as the external actions, is the essential part of conduct. When the will has been distinctly present—even if actions do not occur because of some obstruction—we can call this conduct. In contrast, when the will is not sufficiently present, even if there are actions, we cannot say there is conduct. When the internal activity of consciousness flourishes, the will arises, its goal being from the outset an event in consciousness. We can call this conduct as well. Although psychologists make a distinction between internal and external, all phenomena of consciousness have the same character.

I have discussed how the process of the will is a necessary part of conduct, and I now want to go a step farther and explain both the character of the will as a phenomenon of consciousness and the position it occupies in consciousness. From the perspective of psychology, the will is an activity that unifies ideas, and as such it must be a type of apperception. Two types of activity join ideas in consciousness. In one, the cause of the union of ideas is found primarily in conditions of the external world, with the direction of the union unclear in consciousness and therefore felt to be passive; this type of activity is called association. In the other, the cause of the union of ideas is found in consciousness, with the direction of the union clearly conscious and thus felt to be actively united; this second type of activity is called apperception. As I said before, the will initially involves an idea of a goal that determines the direction of the union of ideas and on the basis of this we construct— from the various ideas of movement that we have previously acquired from experience—a union of ideas that is appropriate for the realization of the self; therefore, the will is an apperceptive activity. The fact that the will is an activity of the unity of ideas becomes all the more evident in a conflict of desires. What we call a decision is nothing more than the conclusion of the unity.

How does the activity of apperception in the will relate to other activities of apperception? Like the will, the activities of thinking and imagination are activities of apperception. In these activities, a certain unifying idea constitutes a foundation upon which the activities unify concepts in ways that suit their goals; hence the activities are identical to the will in terms of the role of ideas. Because the goals of the unities are different and the laws of unity are therefore also different, these apperceptive activities are thought to be distinct activities of consciousness. Let us investigate in greater detail the points in which they are different and in which they are the same.

When we compare imagination and the will we discover that the goal of imagination is the imitation of nature and that the goal of the will is movement. Consequently, imagination unifies ideas so that they accord with the true state of nature, whereas the will unifies ideas so that they accord with the desires of the self. Prior to the movement of the will we necessarily imagine the movement one time; in imagining something in nature, we must first become that thing and then think. Because imagination always concerns external things with which one cannot be completely congruent, they are felt to be other than oneself. Imagining a certain thing and acting on it are inevitably seen as different. With this further thought, however, we find that this is a quantitative, not qualitative difference. As in an artist's imagination, if we attain to the realm of inspiration, we totally submerge the self in the thing; consequently the self and the thing are in complete congruence, and we feel the action of the thing to be the activity of our own will.

This brings us to thinking and the will. The goal of thinking is truth, and the laws that control the linkage of ideas in thinking are the laws of logic. In contrast, we do not necessarily will that which we take to be truth, and we do not think that what we will is necessarily truth. Moreover, the unity of thinking is simply the unity of abstract concepts, whereas the unities of the will and imagination are unities of concrete ideas. In these respects, at a glance there is a distinction between thinking and the will, and no one confuses the two, but with careful consideration we see that this is not an obvious or indisputable distinction. A sufficient reason is always concealed behind the will. Even if this reason is not perfect, the will always functions on the basis of a certain truth—that is, the will is established by thinking. In reverse, as in Wang Yang-ming's emphasis on the identity of knowledge and action,[1] true knowledge is

---

1. Wang Yang-ming (1472–1528), also known as Wang Shou-jen, was a Neo-Confucion philosopher and statesman who advanced a view of original goodness, an innate sense of right and wrong, and the unity of knowledge and action. He states in a discussion about putting filial piety into practice: "There have never been people who know but do not act. Those who are supposed to know but do not act simply do not yet know." William Theodore DeBary, Wing-Tsit Chan, and Burton Watson, eds., *Sources of Chinese Tradition*, vol.1 (New York: Columbia University Press, 1960), 524.

always accompanied by the performance of the will. To think in a certain way but not to desire in the same way means that one does not yet truly know.

We thus see that the apperceptions of thinking, imagination, and the will are fundamentally identical unifying activities. Thinking and imagination are the unifying activities of ideas that pertain to all aspects of the self and of other things, whereas the will is the unifying activity of ideas that pertain only to the action of the self. The former are merely idealistic—that is, possible—unities, whereas the latter is an actual unity, a culmination of unity.

I have outlined the status of the will in the activity of apperception, so let us now consider the relation between the will and other unions of ideas, such as association and fusion. As I stated before with regard to association, the factor that determines the direction of the union of ideas exists in the external world, not in the internal world. I discussed this as a matter of degree, however—we cannot say that there is no unifying activity within association. It is simply that this activity does not appear clearly in consciousness. The union is even more unconscious in an amalgamation of ideas—we are not conscious even of the activity of amalgamation—but this does not mean that there is no internal unity. In short, all phenomena of consciousness possess the same form as the will, and in a certain sense they are the will. If we call the unifying power at the base of these unifying activities the self, then the will is the activity that most clearly expresses the self. Indeed, it is in the action of the will that we are most clearly conscious of our selves.

CHAPTER 16

Conduct (11)

I have discussed conduct as a phenomenon of consciousness from the perspective of psychology, and now I will address such issues as the origin of the unifying power of the will at the base of conduct and the significance of this power in reality. This calls for philosophical clarification of the character of the will and conduct.

From what does the unity of the will, which unifies ideas internally by virtue of a certain fixed goal, arise in us? From the scientist's standpoint that there is no existence apart from matter, we would conclude that the unifying power arises from our bodies. Like those of animals, our bodies are organisms that constitute systems. Regardless of the presence or absence of spirit, animals can perform various mechanically-ordered movements—reflexive movements, automatic movements, and more complex instinctual acts—through the central nervous system. Human will developed from these unconscious movements. Even now, when the will is trained it returns to the state of these unconscious movements; we consequently think that these movements are all of the same type and that they all occur by means of the same power. The various goals of organisms serve the maintenance and development of life in the individual or in its species, and the goal of our will, too, is the preservation of life; it is only because we are conscious of it in the will that this goal seems different from the others. It is in terms of this goal of life that scientists try to explain elevated human spiritual demands.

It is difficult, however, to locate the basis of the will in material force and to explain the subtle and profound demands of human life merely in terms of the desire to live. Even if the development of a lofty will accompanies the flourishing of life functions, the highest goal lies in the former, not in the latter. Contrary to what we might think, the latter is the means to the former. Leaving this argument for later, I want to consider another issue: if we follow scientists and regard the will as emerging from the physical activity of organisms, then what sort of capability must we assume matter possesses?

There are two perspectives from which we can argue that the teleological movement of organisms arises from matter: from the first perspective, nature is considered to be teleological, and a latent purposeful power—similar to the power functioning in the seeds of living things—is held to exist in matter; from the second, matter is regarded as possessing only a mechanical power, and apparently purposeful natural phenomena all are held to occur fortuitously. Strict scientists work from the latter perspective, but I think that the two perspectives are the same, for they never diverge fundamentally. Even in the latter, we must assume a power that brings about certain fixed, unchanging phenomena. We must make the assumption that for mechanical movement to occur there must be a power of generation latent in matter. Can we not hold that, for the same reason, there is latent in matter a purposeful power like that found in organisms? Some people advance an explanation of the purposeful movements of organisms in terms of simpler physical and chemical laws, without hypothesizing such a power. By extension, the laws of contemporary physics and chemistry can perhaps be explained by a still simpler law—or, rather, because the advance of knowledge is infinite, they necessarily will be explained in this way. From this perspective, truth is merely relative.

In opposition to this perspective, I deem it correct to place a greater emphasis on synthesis than on analysis and to view purposeful nature as advancing through stages from individual differentiation to a greater synthesis, thereby displaying its true meaning.

According to a view of reality mentioned earlier, "material body" is simply a name attached to an unchanging relationship between phenomena of consciousness, so it is not that material bodies give rise to consciousness but that consciousness creates material bodies. Even the most objective mechanical movement is established by our logical unity and thus never separates from the unity of consciousness. It develops and becomes a phenomenon in the life of a living thing; further, it becomes a phenomenon of consciousness in an animal, and in this way its unity becomes increasingly active, multi-faceted, and profound. Will is the deepest unifying power of our consciousness and also the most profound expression of the unifying power of reality. That which is regarded from the outside as a mere mechanical movement or a process of living phenomena is, in its true internal significance, the will. Just as what we might take to be mere wood or stone is, in its true significance, a statue of a compassionate, perfected Buddha or of a brave *deva* king, nature is an expression of the will, and it is through our will that we can grasp the true significance of profound nature. Of course, if we were to divide phenomena into internal and external and consequently see mental and physical phenomena as totally separate, we would perhaps consider this theory a mere fancy; but the concrete facts of direct experience contain no distinctions between internal and external and, contrary to what one might think, my view indicates a direct fact.

The above perspective coincides with that of scientists who believe that the mechanical movement of material bodies and the purposefulness of organisms share the same base as the will and that the activities of material bodies, organisms, and the will are identical. But what scientists regard as constituting the base of these activities is diametrically opposed to what I see: they regard material force as the base, whereas I focus on the will.

In my analysis of conduct I have taken the will and action to be two different things, but their relationship is not one of cause and effect, for they are the two sides of one and the same thing. Action is the expression of the will, and that which is regarded from without as action can be regarded from within as the will.

CHAPTER 17

The Freedom of the Will

I argued in the last chapter that in psychological terms the will is simply one phenomenon of consciousness but that in terms of its fundamental nature it is the base of reality. We now must consider whether the will is a free or determined activity, a question that has perplexed scholars since ancient times and that holds important implications for morality. Through this discussion we can clarify the philosophical character of the will.

Judging from what people usually believe, we all consider the will to be free. Given our experience of our consciousness, within a certain sphere of action we are able to do something while also being able not to do it—that is, we believe we are free within that sphere. For this reason ideas of responsibility, irresponsibility, self-confidence, regret, praise, and blame arise in us. But let us now give careful thought to what is meant by "within a certain sphere."

We cannot freely control all things in the external world. Even our own bodies cannot be freely manipulated in any absolute sense. The voluntary movement of muscles seems to be free, but if we become ill we are no longer able to move our muscles freely. The only things we can freely manage are our own phenomena of consciousness. Even so, we have neither the freedom to create ideas anew nor the freedom to recall at any time something we once experienced. That which we regard as truly free is simply the activity of a union of ideas—that is, how we analyze ideas and how we synthesize them derives from the freedom of the self. And yet, an indisputable, a priori law functions in the analysis and synthesis of ideas, so we are not here able to do as we please either. Moreover, when a union of ideas stands alone or when a certain union is especially strong, we must fully obey it. We possess total freedom of choice only in the context of the a priori law of the establishment of ideas, and only when of two or more ways to unite ideas none has the strength to dominate.

Many of those who expound theories about the freedom of the will base their arguments on the facts of experience in the internal world. According to them, within that scope the selection of motives is in all respects a matter of our freedom and has no other reason than ourselves. They argue that decision is based on a type of mystical power—called the will—that is independent of both the various conditions in the external world and disposition, habit, and character in the internal world. In short, they posit a power that exists apart from the union of ideas while controlling it.

In contrast, those who expound deterministic theories of the will generally do so on the basis of observations of facts in the external world. According to them, the phenomena of the universe do not occur fortuitously; even extremely minute matters, when investigated in detail, necessarily possess a sufficient cause. This is the idea behind scholarly inquiry, and with the development of science it becomes increasingly certain. The causes and effects of natural phenomena formerly considered mysterious have since become clear, and we have advanced to the point where we can calculate them mathematically. At present, only our will is still regarded as having no cause. Even the will, however, cannot escape from the great, unchanging laws of nature. We continue to think that the will is free because the development of science is still in its infancy and because we cannot explain each of the causes of the will. It is true that in individual instances the action of the will appears to be irregular and devoid of any fixed cause, but if we look statistically at the actions of a large number of people, we discern that the actions are surprisingly orderly and that they have certain causes and effects. These observations strengthen our conviction that there are causes related to our will and bring us to the conclusion that our will, just like all other phenomena of nature, is ruled by a necessary, mechanical law of cause and effect and therefore is not some sort of mysterious power.

Which of these opposing theories is correct? As I stated before, those who uphold theories of free will in an extreme form tell us that we have a mysterious ability to choose motives freely without any cause or reason. But this assertion is totally mistaken, for there must be a sufficient reason for our choice of motives. Even if the reason does not appear clearly in consciousness, it must exist beneath consciousness. Moreover, if—as the proponents of free will contend—something decides things fortuitously without any reason, then at the time of decision we would not feel that the will is free; rather we would feel the decision to be a fortuitous event that has functioned from without, and our feeling of responsibility for the decision would be weak. Those who advance theories of free will set forth their arguments on the basis of experience in the internal world, but such internal experience actually proves the opposite—determinism.

Let us now offer a criticism of the determinist argument. These proponents claim that because natural phenomena are controlled by the law of mechanical necessity, phenomena of consciousness must be controlled by it as well. This stance is based on the assumption that phenomena of consciousness and natural phenomena (that is, material phenomena) are identical and controlled by the same law. But is this assumption correct? Whether phenomena of consciousness and material phenomena are controlled by the same law is an unsettled issue, and arguments marshalled on this assumption are extremely weak. Even if modern physiological psychology advances to the point where we can physically or chemically explain each of the functions of the brain at the base of consciousness, will we thereby be able to assert that phenomena of consciousness are controlled by a mechanical law of necessity? For example, the bronze that serves as the raw material of a statue perhaps cannot escape the domination of the laws of mechanical necessity, but can we not say that the meaning expressed by the statue exists apart from those laws? So-called spiritual meaning cannot be seen, heard, or counted; it transcends the laws of mechanical necessity.

In summary, the kind of will described by those who argue for the freedom of the will—a will that is totally without cause or reason—does not exist. Such a contingent will would not be felt to be free; rather, it would be felt to be oppressive. When we function for a certain reason, that is, from the internal character of the self, we feel ourselves to be free. And we feel most free when the cause of a motive emerges from the most profound internal character of the self. The reason behind the will, however, is not a mechanical cause as described by determinists. Our spirit contains a law governing its activity, and when spirit functions in accordance with its own law, it is truly free.

Freedom thus has two possible meanings: (1) being totally without cause, that is, fortuitous or contingent, and (2) having no external restrictions and therefore functioning of and by oneself. The latter indicates autonomous freedom, and this is the freedom of the will. At this point, the following problem arises. Assuming that freedom means to function according to one's character, we see that amongst the countless things around us nothing fails to function so. The flowing of water and the burning of fire are examples of this. Why then is only the will considered to be free and other things to be determined?

The occurrence of a phenomenon in the natural world is determined strictly by its circumstances. Only one, certain phenomenon—and no others—arises from a particular set of circumstances. All natural phenomena arise according to this sort of blind necessity. Phenomena of consciousness, however, do not simply arise, for they are phenomena of which we are conscious—that is, they arise and we know that they have arisen. Knowing something or being conscious of it includes other possibilities. To be conscious of taking something includes the possibility of not taking it. To put it more exactly, consciousness always possesses a universal character—consciousness always includes an idealistic element, otherwise it is not consciousness. That consciousness has such a character means that it harbors possibilities other than actual events. Being actual yet including ideals, being idealistic and yet not separating from actuality—this is the distinctive character of consciousness. Consciousness is in fact never controlled by other things, for it is always controlling them. Knowing this, even if our conduct occurs according to necessary laws we are not confined by the conduct. Moreover, actuality is simply one particular instance of the ideals that constitute the base of consciousness;

that is, it is simply one process in which the ideals actualize themselves. Conduct therefore is not generated from without, but from within. And because we see actuality as simply one instance of the ideals, consciousness comes to include numerous other possibilities.

Consciousness is free not because it functions fortuitously beyond the laws of nature, but rather because it follows its own nature. It is free not because it functions for no reason, but because it knows well the reasons behind its functioning. As our knowledge advances, we become freer people. Even if we are controlled or oppressed by others, when we know this we extricate ourselves from the oppression. If we go even farther and realize the unavoidable reason for the situation, then the oppression turns into freedom—Socrates was freer than the Athenians who poisoned him. Pascal said that a person is as weak as a reed, but because he or she is a thinking reed, even if the whole world tries to destroy him, he is greater than that which kills him, for he himself knows that he will die.

As discussed earlier in the section on reality, the idealistic element— that is, the unifying activity—that constitutes the base of consciousness is not a product of nature; rather, it is because of this unity that nature comes to exist. This unity is the infinite power at the base of reality, and it cannot be limited quantitatively. It exists independently of the necessary laws of nature. Because our will is an expression of that power, it is free and goes beyond the control of such natural laws.

CHAPTER 18

A Study of Conduct in Terms of Value

We can examine all phenomena or events in two ways. One is the investigation of their cause or reason, that is, how they occurred and why they must be as they are. The other is the investigation of goals, that is, the purpose for which they occurred. Let us imagine for example that here is a flower. If someone asks how it came into being, we must answer that it arose in accordance with botanical and environmental conditions and in accordance with the laws of physics and chemistry. Now if someone asks about the purpose for which it occurred, we would answer that it arose to produce fruit. The former approach constitutes theoretical inquiry into the laws of the establishment of things, whereas the latter constitutes practical inquiry into the laws of the activity of things.

With regard to phenomena of the so-called inorganic world, we can ask how they arose but not for what purpose they arose, so it must be said that they have no goal. One can, however, argue that the goal and the cause in this case are identical. For example, if we hit a billiard ball with a certain force in a specific direction, it will undoubtedly roll in that fixed direction, but the ball has no goal. The person who hit the ball might have a goal, but it is not a goal internal to the ball; the ball is moved of necessity in accordance with causes in the external world. But from another point of view, the ball moves in a fixed direction precisely because there is such a power of movement in the ball itself. In terms of the internal force of the ball, we can view the movement as a purposeful activity of self-actualization.

When we advance to plants and animals, the internal goal of the self becomes clear and the cause and the goal can be distinguished. The phenomena that occur in plants and animals do so according to inevitable physical and chemical laws. These phenomena are not insignificant, for their goal is the existence and development of the entire living thing. In these phenomena, however, that which has occurred as the result of a certain cause is not necessarily purposeful, for sometimes the goal of the whole and that of certain phenomena—which are parts of the whole— come into conflict. In this regard we must pursue axiological study of the phenomena and ask what kinds of phenomena coincide most with the goal of the whole.

We can regard the unifying goal of non-human living things as a figment of imagination added by us from without and thereby do away with it. That is, we can regard the phenomena of living things as meaningless unions established by the collection of a certain amount of energy. Only when we come to our phenomena of consciousness can we stop viewing things in this way. From the outset, no phenomenon of consciousness is a union of insignificant elements, for each is a single, unifying activity. If we were to remove this unifying activity from the activity of thinking, imagination, and the will, we would destroy them. The first issue we must address concerning these activities is not how they arise, but rather how one should think, how one should imagine, and how one should act. We thus come to the study of logic, aesthetics, and ethics.

Certain scholars attempt to derive laws of value from laws of existence. But I do not think we can derive value judgments about things from the fact that one thing arises from another. We cannot explain through the law of cause and effect, which holds that a red flower gives rise to a certain effect and a blue flower gives rise to another effect, why it is that one flower is beautiful and another ugly, or why one possesses great value and the other does not. In order to make such value judgments, there must be another law that serves as a standard. Once thinking, imagination, and the will have occurred in terms of facts, then our thinking, no matter how mistaken, our will, no matter how perverse, and our imagination, no matter how lacking, all arise according to sufficient causes. Both the will to murder people and the will to save them arise from certain necessary causes and produce inevitable effects and, in this respect, neither has the slightest superiority or inferiority. Only when there are such standards as the demands of the conscience or life desires does there arise a significant difference of superiority and inferiority between these two types of conduct.

Some theorists argue that what gives great pleasure has great value and contend that they have thus been able to derive the law of value from the law of cause and effect. But we cannot explain merely from the law of cause and effect why a certain result gives us pleasure and why another does not. What kinds of things we like and what kinds we hate are facts of direct experience that have a basis different from the law of cause and effect. Psychologists state that whatever increases our life force is pleasure. But is this the case? Is it not true that pessimists feel that living is the source of pain? Other theorists argue that powerful things possess value. To the human mind, what sort of thing is most powerful? It is not necessarily materially powerful things but the things that most move our desires—the things that have value for us—that are most powerful. The possession or lack of power is determined according to value; value is not determined according to power.

All of our desires and demands are unexplainable, given facts. It is said that we eat in order to live, but "in order to live" is an explanation added after the fact. Our appetite does not arise for such a reason. An infant's first drinking of milk is not so it can live: the infant drinks for the sake of drinking. Our desires and demands are not only unexplainable facts of direct experience but also, contrary to what one might think, the secret keys by which we are able to understand the true meaning of reality. A complete explanation of reality must explain not only how things exist, but also why they exist.

CHAPTER 19

Theories of Ethics (1)

I have already discussed some of what is involved in the study of conduct in terms of value, so let us now examine the good. As stated before, we all make value judgments about our conduct, and I now want to discuss such ethical problems as where the standard for ethical judgment lies, what sort of conduct is good, and what sort of conduct is bad. These are the most important problems we face. No one can ignore them. In both the East and the West, ethics is one of the oldest fields of learning, and since long ago many theories of ethics have been developed. I will present a broad outline of the main schools of ethics, evaluate them, and expound my own ethical theory.

We can broadly categorize traditional systems of ethics by two main theories: the first is the heteronomous ethical theory, which locates the standard of good and evil in authority apart from humanity; the second is the autonomous ethical theory, which locates this standard in human nature. In addition to these main theories, there is another broad grouping of ethical theories called the intuitive theory. This theory includes various subdivisions, some falling under the heteronomous ethical theory and others under the autonomous theory. Let us start with the intuitive theory and then move on to the others.

The intuitive theory includes a variety of positions, but it generally claims that the moral laws that regulate our conduct are intuitively clear and have no reason apart from themselves. What kind of behavior is good and what kind is bad can be known intuitively, just as when we know that fire is hot and water is cold. The good and evil in conduct moreover pertain to the character of conduct itself and cannot be explained on the basis of separate reasons or standards. If we examine our daily experience, we see that to judge good and evil in conduct is not to think of this or that reason but, in general, to judge intuitively. We possess a conscience, and just as the eye judges the beauty and ugliness of things, we can judge directly the good and evil in conduct. The intuitive theory bases itself on this fact; it is the theory closest to the "facts." Further, to say that good and evil in conduct cannot be explained in terms of separate reasons is highly effective in maintaining the dignity of morality.

Although the intuitive theory is simple and effective in practice, how much value does it have as a theory of ethics? According to this theory, what is intuitively clear is not the ultimate goal of human nature but the laws of conduct. The intuitive theory includes two views: one maintains that the good or evil in conduct is intuitively evident in individual cases, the other maintains that the fundamental moral law that encompasses all individual moral judgments is intuitively clear. Either way, the heart of the intuitive theory consists of the idea that there is a directly self-evident law of conduct.

In the moral judgments of everyday conduct, that is, in the dictates of the conscience, can we find the directly self-evident—and therefore accurate and contradictionless—moral law set forth by the intuitive theory? When we look at individual cases, we see that there are no such clear and accurate judgments. In certain situations we are confused in our judgments of good and evil; at one point we consider something correct and then later deem it false. Even in a single situation, judgments of good and evil differ greatly depending on the person. No critical thinker can hold that there are precise moral judgments in individual cases. But what about general cases? Do the self-evident principles discussed by intuitive theorists really exist? In fact, these principles differ from person to person and therefore are never consistent—this offers proof that no self-evident principle can be universally acknowledged. We moreover cannot find such principles among what any given society considers self-evident duties. Such things as loyalty and filial piety certainly are natural duties, but various conflicts and changes arise between them, thus we can never clearly know what sort of thing true loyalty or filial piety might be. Further, even when we consider the meaning of wisdom, bravery, benevolence, and justice, we cannot say what sort of wisdom or bravery is the true one, nor can we say that all wisdom or bravery is good, for they can be used toward evil ends. Of the four, benevolence and justice are closest to being self-evident principles, but benevolence is not absolutely good in all cases, for unwarranted benevolence can result in evil. Also, even though we speak of justice, it is never clear what constitutes true justice—for example, in our dealings with people, what is the correct way of acting? A simple equality of all people is not justice, because treating people according to their individual value constitutes part of justice. And assuming that we are to treat people according to their value, what determines their value? The point I am making is that in our moral judgments we do not possess even one of the self-evident principles referred to by the intuitive theorists. That which is considered a self-evident principle is simply a proposition that repeats contentless words with the same meaning.

As I argued before, if we cannot prove the intuition of good and evil in the way that it is advanced by proponents of the intuitive theory, then the intuitive approach has little value as a theory. But if we assume for the sake of argument that such intuition exists and that the good is to follow the laws provided by that intuition, then what sort of ethical theory does the intuitive theory become? As these theorists contend, intuition cannot be explained by reason, for it is a totally direct and meaning-free consciousness that is unrelated to feelings of pain and pleasure or to likes and dislikes. So if we assume that following such intuition is good, then the good to us is meaningless, and to follow it is to engage in blind obedience. The moral law then becomes something oppressive that is imposed on human nature from without, and the intuitive theory amounts to a type of heteronomous ethics.

Many intuitive theorists of course do not emphasize intuition in this heteronomous sense. They see intuition as identical to reason; that is, they think that the fundamental laws of morality are self-evident because of reason. From their perspective, to do good is to follow reason, and thus the distinction between good and evil cannot be clarified through intuition but can be explained by reason. Certain intuitive theorists view intuition as identical with pleasure and displeasure or likes and dislikes. From this perspective, the good is good because it gives a sort of pleasure or satisfaction and therefore the standard of good and evil shifts according to the degree of pleasure or satisfaction.

In these ways, depending on the meaning of "intuition," the intuitive theory approaches a number of other ethical theories. Of course, an intuitive theory in its pure sense must signify an intuition devoid of any meaning, but like heteronomous ethics, such an ethical theory fails to explain why we must follow the good. The basis of morality becomes something completely contingent and meaningless. Fundamentally, what we call moral intuition actually includes various principles, including heteronomous principles derived from an authority that is wholly other than oneself and principles deriving from reason, feeling, and desire. This is why the "self-evident principles" of the intuitive theory fall into various contradictions and conflicts. There is no way we can construct a sound theory on such confused principles.

CHAPTER 20

Theories of Ethics (11)

I have discussed the imperfection of the intuitive theory of ethics and shown how, depending on the meaning of intuition, it amounts to various other theories. I will now discuss a purely heteronomous ethics—the authority theory. Proponents of this theory observe that moral good differs from such demands of human nature as the pleasure or satisfaction of the self, and that the good has a sense of being a strict command. They argue that morality derives from the commands of that which has absolute authority and power over us, and so we should follow the laws of morality not for the advantage of the self, but simply for the sake of following the orders of that absolute authority. They also hold that good and evil are determined by the commands of the authority figure. Because the basis of all our moral judgments is cultivated by instruction from our teachers and parents, laws, social systems, and mores, it is only natural for such an ethical theory to arise. In contrast to the orders of the conscience put forth by the intuitive ethical theory, this theory emphasizes authority in the external world.

In the authority theory, the external authority figure must be something with absolute authority and power over us. We find the appearance of two types of authority theories in the history of ethics: (1) the monarchical authority theory, based on a sovereign ruler, and (2) the divine authority theory, based on God. The latter was practiced in the Middle Ages when Christianity possessed supreme power. According to such proponents as Duns Scotus,[1] God has infinite power over us, and God's will is totally free. God neither commands us to do something because it is good nor acts in accordance with reason, for God transcends such restrictions. In other words, God does not command things because they are good—they are good because God commands them. Duns Scotus takes this theory to an extreme, arguing that if God were to command a massacre, the massacre would be good.

A prominent advocate of the monarchical authority theory is Thomas Hobbes, an Englishman who wrote at the beginning of the modern era. According to Hobbes, human nature is totally evil, and in nature the strong prey on the weak. We can escape the suffering caused by this state of affairs only by handing over all authority to one monarch and then fully obeying the monarch's commands. Hobbes argues that to obey the monarch's commands is good, while to disobey is bad. We see a similar type of authority theory in the thought of the Chinese philosopher Hsün-tzu,[2] who wrote that the good is to follow the way of ancient kings.

What sort of conclusion do we reach if we argue strictly from the standpoint of the authority theory? We cannot explain why we must do the good. This unexplainability constitutes precisely the gist of the theory. We obey the authority figure simply because it is authoritative. If we obey the authority for a different reason, we will no longer be obeying

1. John Duns Scotus (1266–1308), a Scottish philosopher and theologian, regarded the love of God as a fundamental moral principle.

2. Hsün-tzu (298–338 B.C.E.) argued that humans are inherently "evil" in the sense of selfishly desiring profit and sensual pleasure; learning and training serve to control these innate tendencies and to help cultivate good people. Hsün-tzu believed that, given our basic nature, a strong ruler modelled after the ancient sage-kings of China is needed to control and punish people in society.

because of the authority. Some say that fear is the most appropriate motive for obeying authority, but behind the fear lies consideration of the advantages and disadvantages of the self; if we obey for the sake of these advantages and disadvantages, however, we are no longer obeying because of the authority. For this reason such thinkers as Hobbes diverge from the standpoint of the pure authority theory.

According to Kirchmann,[3] who set forth the authority theory most provocatively in recent times, when we encounter something with great power, like a high mountain or an immense ocean, we are struck by its power and experience awe. This feeling is not a state of fear or pain, but the state in which the self becomes captivated by something majestic in the external world, surrenders itself, and merges with it. If the entity with great power has will, it elicits a feeling of reverence. According to Kirchmann, the motive for obeying authority is a feeling of reverence. But if we think about this carefully, we see that our reverence for another is not groundless: we revere the person as someone who has realized the ideals we ourselves have been unable to realize. We therefore do not revere merely the person—we revere the ideals as well. This is why wild animals find no value in Śākyamuni or Confucius.

In strict authority theory, then, morality amounts to blind subservience. Both fear and reverence are completely meaningless, blind emotions. In one of Aesop's fables, a fawn sees its mother flee in fear when a dog barks; the fawn asks why she, having a large body, ran at the sound of a small dog. The doe answers that she fled because the bark of the dog was terribly frightening, though she knew not why. Such meaningless fear appears to be the most appropriate moral motive in the authority theory. If this is the case, then morality and knowledge are polar opposites, and the ignorant are the good. It would follow, then, that for humans to progress and develop, they must rid themselves of the restrictions of morality as soon as possible. It would also follow that when we act in a certain way because of a realization that we ought to do so rather than from a sense of obeying the commands of authority, we fall short of morally good conduct.

In the framework of the authority theory, then, we cannot explain moral motives, and the so-called moral law is nearly meaningless; as a result, the distinction between good and evil loses any possible standard.

---

3. Julius Hermann von Kirchmann (1802–84) wrote on Spinoza, Locke, Hume, Leibniz, and Kant's *Critiques*.

Some might argue that we should blindly obey something simply because it has authority, but there are various types of authority. For example, we may encounter violent authority and high spiritual authority, but because in either case we obey authority, no difference is realized and a standard of good and evil cannot be established. Of course, the magnitude of power might be deemed a standard, but we can discuss this only after determining our ideals. Our answer to the question of who is stronger, Jesus or Napoleon, depends on how we set our ideals. If we say that the powerful are those who possess power in the external world, then those with physical power are most powerful.

Saigyō[4] exclaimed, "Though I know not what is enshrined, my tears flow in the face of its awesomeness." The majesty of morality dwells in an unfathomable realm. Although the authority theory contains an element of truth in its focus on this point, its great defect lies in its consequent forgetting of the natural demands rooted in human nature. Morality is based on original human nature, and why one must perform the good must be explained on this basis.

4. See note 14 for "Upon Resetting the Type" in the Preface.

CHAPTER 21

Theories of Ethics (III)

Because theories of heteronomous ethics cannot explain why we must perform the good, the good loses all meaning. This leads us to seek the basis of morality in human nature and then to consider in terms of human nature such problems as the good and the reason we must perform the good. Ethical systems that take this approach are called autonomous ethics and can be divided into three main types: the first, based on reason, is called the rational or intellectual theory; the second, based on the feelings of pain and pleasure, is called the hedonic theory; and the third, based on the action of the will, is called the activity theory.

The rational or intellectual theory of ethics (dianoetic ethics) identifies good and evil or right and wrong in morality with truth and falsehood in knowledge. It holds that the true nature of things is, namely, the good, that if one knows the true aspect of things one sees clearly by oneself what one must do, and that our duty can be deduced like a geometric truth. According to this theory, we must perform the good because the good is truth. We humans are provided with the faculty of reason, and just as we must follow rational principles in knowledge, so we must follow them in practice, too. (As a word of caution, let me add that although *reason*[1] has a variety of philosophical meanings, here it indicates the relation of abstract concepts in the usual sense.) On the one hand, in opposition to Hobbes's view that the moral law is something arbitrary that can be swayed by the will of the monarch, the rational theory contends that the moral law is inherent in the character of things and is eternal and unchanging. On the other hand, the rational theory holds that when we seek the basis of good and evil in such receptivity as perception or feeling, we cannot explain the universality of the moral law, and that in taking that approach we have to destroy the dignity of duty and make the preferences of each person the sole criterion. On the basis of the universality of reason, then, this theory attempts to set forth the universality of the moral law and to establish the dignity of duty. Although this theory is often conflated with the intuitive theory, I think it best to consider them separately, for intuition is not necessarily limited to the intuition of reason.

The purest example of the rational theory is Samuel Clarke's approach,[2] in which relations between things in the human world are held to be as clear as mathematical principles, and by means of these relations we can know the suitability or unsuitability of things. This means, for example, that because God is infinitely superior to us, we must obey God; or that the unjust things others do to us are still unjust when we do them in return. Clarke also discusses why humans must perform the good, arguing that rational animals must follow reason. At times he even states that people who try to work in opposition to justice are like those who desire to change the character of things, and in this way Clarke totally confuses the "is" with the "ought."

Although the rational theory can clarify the universality of the moral

---

1. The Japanese term used here for "reason" is *ri*.

2. Samuel Clarke (1675–1729), an English philosopher and rationalist theologian, set forth an ethical theory in terms of fitness (suitability) in the relations between things.

law and lead us to take duty seriously, it does not provide a way to explain all of morality. We must ask whether we can know, in an a priori manner through the power of formal understanding, the moral law that guides our conduct. The power of formal understanding provides only laws, such as the so-called three laws of thought in logic—it cannot give any content. Exponents of the rational theory like to give examples from geometry, but geometric axioms are not elucidated solely through the power of formal understanding; rather, they derive from the character of space. The deductive inferences of geometry result from applying the laws of logic to a fundamental intuition of the character of space. Like-wise, in ethics, we must proceed according to the laws of logic in order to apply fundamental principles after they have become clear, but it is not the case that the principles have been clarified by those laws. For example, is the moral law "Love thy neighbor" clear simply by virtue of the power of understanding? We manifest characteristics of altruism as well as characteristics of self-love. But why is one superior to the other? It is not the power of understanding that determines which is superior, but our feelings and desires. Even if our intellects could enable us to know the true character of things, this would not give us knowledge of what the good is. The fact that a thing *is* a certain way does not enable us to know that it *ought to be* a certain way. Though Clarke contends that we can know suitability and unsuitability from the true character of things, judgments of suitability and unsuitability are not really judgments by the pure intellect but rather value judgments. Only when we seek something do judgments of suitability and unsuitability occur.

Exponents of the rational theory offer an explanation for why we must perform the good by arguing that we must follow rational principles because we are rational beings. It is only natural for someone who under-stands rational principles to follow them in the domain of knowledge. But logical judgment and the choices of the will are different matters. Logical judgments do not necessarily become causes of the will—the will arises from feelings or impulses, not from mere abstract logic. Even Con-fucius's maxim, "Do not do unto others what you would not have others do unto you," is nearly meaningless without the motivation of sympathy. If abstract logic were the motivation of the will, then those who are most adept at reasoning would be the best people. No one can deny, however, that ignorant people are sometimes actually better than those who have knowledge.

I discussed Clarke earlier as an advocate of the rational theory. He represents the theoretical side of that perspective, whereas the Cynics[3] represent its practical side. Basing their argument on Socrates' claim that the good and knowledge are identical, the Cynics regard all desire and pleasure as evil and conclude that the only good is to rid oneself of desire and pleasure and to follow reason. But their pure reason—a contentless, passive reason—merely stands in opposition to desire. For the Cynics, the goal of morality lies in overcoming desire and pleasure and in maintaining the freedom of spirit. The renowned Diogenes[4] is a good example of this approach.

The Stoics, who succeeded the Cynics, set forth similar principles:[5] the universe is controlled by reason, they stated, and the essence of humanity is found in this rationality. To follow this reason is to follow the laws of nature, and this is the only good in human life. Life, health, and possessions are not good, and poverty, suffering, disease, and death are not evil. For the Stoics, the highest good is found only in the freedom and tranquility of the mind. For this reason the Stoics, like the Cynics, attempt to eliminate all desire and to achieve desirelessness (*Apathie*). Epictetus is a key representative of this view.

When we follow the Cynics and the Stoics and take pure reason, as opposed to desire, for our goal, we can neither provide a theoretical articulation of moral motivation nor in practice give active content to the good. All we can do is to assert, like the Cynics and Stoics did, that ridding oneself of desire is the only good. But it is only because we seek an even greater good that we have to rid ourselves of desire. Nothing is more irrational than to say that the good is to control desire just for the sake of controlling desire.

3. This school of Greek philosophy was started by Antisthenes (455–360 B.C.E.), a student of Socrates. Cynics argue that happiness originates in total freedom from desire.

4. The life of Diogenes (413–327 B.C.E.) illustrates the teachings of the Cynics, especially regarding the virtues of simplicity and self-control. He supposedly lived in a tub at the temple of Cybele, and at midday he searched with a lantern for an honest person. His lifestyle earned him the nickname *Kyon*, or dog.

5. This school of Greek philosophy was established by Zeno of Citium (362–264 B.C.E.). Stoics contend that one should accept one's life situation as a reflection of universal reason and that such a life is supported by detachment from the outside world and by living in accordance with human reason.

CHAPTER 22

Theories of Ethics (IV)

The rational theory of ethics goes a step farther than heteronomous ethics in that it attempts to explain the good in terms of essential human nature. But as I said before, we cannot solve the fundamental problem of why one must perform the good if we base the rational theory simply on formal reason. When we reflect deeply on the self, we see that seeking comfort and avoiding discomfort are natural and undeniable facts of human feeling because the will emerges from feelings of pain and plea- sure. Even when an action appears to be performed for a reason other than pleasure, as when someone dies while practicing benevolence, if we examine what lies behind that action we see that the person is seeking a kind of pleasure after all. The goals of the will ultimately do not exist apart from pleasure, and that we take pleasure to be the goal of human life is a self-evident truth needing no further explanation. It is therefore natural that we encounter an ethical theory that considers pleasure to be the sole goal of human nature and that fashions an explanation of the distinction between moral good and evil accordingly. This theory is called the hedonic theory, and it includes two varieties: egoistic hedonism and universalistic hedonism.

The pleasure of the self is the only goal of human life, according to the theory of egoistic hedonism; even when we act for the sake of other people, we are actually seeking the pleasure of the self. From this perspective, the greatest pleasure of the self is the greatest good. The purest representatives of this theory are the Cyrenaic school and Epicurus[1] in Greece.

Aristippus,[2] the founder of the Cyrenaic school, allows for a spiritual pleasure distinguished from physical pleasure, but he considers all pleasure identical, with greatest pleasure being the good. Because he values active pleasure and holds momentary pleasure in higher regard than life-long pleasure, he is a representative of the purest form of the hedonic theory.

Epicurus argues that all pleasure is identical, that pleasure is the sole good, and that pleasure of any sort is not to be rejected unless it leads to painful consequences. Contrary to Aristippus, Epicurus places more value on life-long pleasure than on momentary pleasure and values passive pleasure—that is, a state without pain—more than active pleasure. For Epicurus, the greatest good is the tranquility of the mind. Even so, his fundamental creed is egoistic hedonism, and he regards the four cardinal virtues of the Greeks—wisdom, moderation, courage, and justice—as the necessary means to the pleasure of the self. For example, justice in itself has no value, but it is necessary to the way by which people refrain from committing offenses against each other and secure happiness. This approach assumes its clearest form in Epicurus' opinions about social life: society is necessary for the benefit of the self, and nations exist only to provide for the safety of the individual. To be able to avoid social encumbrances and at the same time to secure adequate safety is

1. Both the Cyrenaic school and Epicurus (341–270 b.c.e.) argued that pleasure is the goal of life. The Cyrenaic school emphasized prudence as a way to avoid pain. Epicurus stressed pleasure in the sense of freedom from pain. Virtue and simple living are conducive to pleasure, the highest good.

2. Aristippus of Cyrene (445–380 B.C.E.) was a student of Socrates.

the most desirable state of affairs. Epicurus' doctrine is rather like anchoritism[3] for it favors the avoidance of family life as much as possible.

Let us next discuss universalistic hedonism, otherwise known as utilitarianism. In its fundamental principles, this theory is identical with egoistic hedonism, but it differs in that it considers social or public pleasure—rather than individual pleasure—the highest good. The most thoroughgoing representative of this theory is Bentham,[4] according to whom the goal of human life is pleasure, and the good is nothing other than pleasure. All pleasure is identical, differing only in quantity, not quality. (Therefore the pleasure of the game of roulette and the pleasure of sublime poetry are identical.) The value of conduct lies not, as the intuitive theorists contend, in the conduct itself, but in the results of the conduct—that is, conduct that gives rise to great pleasure is good conduct. This leads to the question of what sort of conduct is the best conduct. Because the basic principles of hedonism necessarily lead Bentham to think that the greatest happiness of the majority is rationally a greater pleasure than the greatest happiness of the individual, he argues that the greatest happiness of the majority is the highest good and that the greatest conduct is that which promotes this.

From this theoretical perspective, Bentham also discusses a scientific method to determine the value of conduct and pleasure quantitatively; for example, he believes that we can calculate pleasure according to such standards as intensity, duration, certainty, and uncertainty.

As a hedonistic theory Bentham's standpoint is thoroughly consistent, but it lacks a clear explanation of why the greatest happiness of the majority, rather than that of the individual, must be the highest good. Pleasure necessarily involves a subject who feels the pleasure—there is pleasure precisely because there is that which feels it. And the agent who feels pleasure is in all cases an individual. So why is it that from the basic principles of hedonism Bentham came to place the pleasure of the majority above that of the individual? Mill and others focus on the fact that because humans feel sympathy for others they derive greater pleasure in enjoying something with others than in enjoying it alone—but even in this case, the pleasure that comes from sympathy is not the pleasure of

3. Anchoritism refers to the practice of living in seclusion for religious reasons. The term derives from the Greek verb *anachorein*, to withdraw.

4. Jeremy Bentham (1748–1832), an English philosopher, set forth the goal of utilitarianism as "the greatest good for the greatest number."

others but one's own pleasure, so one's own pleasure is still the only standard.

We must also consider what happens when one's pleasure conflicts with the pleasure of others: can we say from the standpoint of hedonism that even then one must forget one's own pleasure and seek the pleasure of others? As with Epicurus' theory, this theory inevitably becomes a form of selfishness and an unavoidable outcome of hedonism. Bentham and Mill argue forcefully that the pleasure of the self and the pleasure of others coincide, but we cannot even begin to prove this argument in the realm of experiential facts.

I have outlined the main points of hedonic theories; let us now critique them. First, if we accept the fundamental assumption of these theories—that pleasure is the only goal of human life—can we give a sufficient standard of conduct by means of these theories? From the standpoint of strict hedonism, all kinds of pleasure are the same, and the differences they exhibit are only quantitative differences of intensity. If we assume various qualitative differences in pleasure by which value differs, then we would have to acknowledge a value-determining principle other than pleasure. This would conflict with the doctrine that pleasure is the only principle determining the value of conduct.

Coming after Bentham, Mill allows for various qualitative distinctions in pleasure and contends that the superiority and inferiority of two types of pleasure can be easily determined by any person who can equally experience the two. For example, all of us would rather choose to be as dissatisfied as Socrates than to be as satisfied as a pig. Mill asserts that these distinctions derive from the human sense of dignity. This assertion diverges, however, from the standpoint of the hedonic theory, in which no possibility is allowed for the exaltation of one pleasure over another, though one may be less intense than the other.

If we assume, as do Epicurus and Bentham, that pleasures are basically the same and differ only quantitatively, then how can we determine quantitative relations between pleasures and thereby determine the value of conduct? Aristippus and Epicurus do not provide a clear standard—they merely say that we are able to discriminate by means of the intellect. As I mentioned, only Bentham discusses such a standard in detail, but even in a single person the feeling of pleasure changes readily depending on the time and the circumstances, and thus it is not clear whether one pleasure is greater in strength than another. It is also exceedingly difficult to determine correspondences between degrees of intensity and duration.

And if it is difficult to establish a yardstick for pleasure in the case of an individual, it is even harder to calculate the pleasure of others and to determine the extent of pleasure, as attempted in the universalistic form of this theory. People usually think that spiritual pleasures are higher than physical ones; indeed, it appears that the value of pleasure has traditionally been fixed, with honor being more important than wealth and the pleasure of many people more precious than that of the individual. But this standard was established on the basis of observations of various facets of things and not on the basis of the intensity of simple pleasure.

The above discussion assumes that the fundamental principles of hedonism are correct, but even so we find it exceedingly difficult to obtain an accurate standard for determining the value of our conduct. Let us now proceed a step farther and investigate the basic assumptions of hedonism: that all people desire pleasure and that pleasure is the sole objective of human life. Everyone makes such assumptions, but if we think about them we see that they are not true. We must acknowledge that in addition to selfish pleasures people possess elevated altruistic or ideal demands. For example, latent in every person's mind to some extent is the desire to give to loved ones even if that might entail suppressing one's own needs, or the desire to put ideals into practice even if that means one might die. Such motives often express an extraordinary power and may even cause people unintentionally to commit tragic, sacrificial acts.

The idea that humans seek only the pleasure of the self appears to be a penetrating truth, but it is actually far from the facts. Advocates of hedonic theories of course recognize the existence of sacrificial acts, but they think that even when we desire to give to our loved ones or dare to commit sacrificial acts in order to put ideals into practice we are trying to satisfy the desires of the self and therefore we in our true colors are merely seeking our own pleasure. It is a fact that every person in every situation seeks the satisfaction of desires, but we cannot say that a person who seeks this satisfaction is seeking pleasure. Even when we put an ideal into practice through much pain and struggle, a feeling of satisfaction inevitably accompanies this accomplishment. This feeling is certainly a kind of pleasure, but we cannot argue that the sensation of pleasure was from the outset the goal of our action. For such a pleasurable sense of satisfaction to occur, there must first exist in us natural desires. And it is precisely because we have such desires that the pleasure of satisfaction arises when they are fulfilled. Accordingly, to say that all demands take pleasure as their goal because the pleasurable sensation is present when those demands are fulfilled is to confuse cause and effect.

Humans have an innate instinct of altruism. For this reason, loving others gives us unlimited satisfaction. But we cannot say that we love others for our own pleasure. If we harbor the slightest idea that we have acted for our own pleasure, then we cannot feel the satisfaction that derives from altruism. Neither the desire to love others nor the desire to love oneself takes pleasure as its goal. The desires for food and sex, for example, derive from our being driven by a kind of necessity found in our innate instincts rather than from their having pleasure as their goal. The hungry lament the existence of appetite and the brokenhearted detest the existence of love. If pleasure were our sole objective, there would be nothing richer in contradiction than human life. Contrary to what one might think, the road to pleasure opens up before us only when we part from all desires. It is for this reason that Epicurus' argument that the state of affairs devoid of all desire—that is, tranquility of mind—is the greatest pleasure coincides with the ideals of the Stoics, who started with a fundamental principle opposite to his.

Some advocates of hedonic theories argue that what today is considered a natural desire without a goal of pleasure was originally something that consciously sought pleasure but that later, in the life of the individual or in the process of the evolution of living things, became unconscious and secondary nature by means of habit. In other words, natural desires that do not take pleasure as their goal originally constituted a means to acquire pleasure and then through habit became the goal itself. (In this regard, Mill and others often give the example of money.) Indeed, some of our desires become second nature by means of such psychological activity, but not all desires that take something other than pleasure as their goal arise through this process. Our minds, like our bodies, are active from birth, and they include various instincts. The fact that chicks naturally pick up unhulled rice or that ducklings naturally enter the water derives from the same principle. Did these instinctual acts go from being conscious acts to being unconscious habits due to heredity? According to present-day theories of biological evolution, the instincts of living things were not established through this process. Rather, instincts originally were capabilities in the eggs of living things, and the living things possessing the capabilities most suited to circumstances survived and eventually came to exhibit these specific capabilities as instincts.

As discussed above, even though hedonism, compared with the rational theory, is closer to the reality of human nature, from the standpoint of hedonism the distinction between good and evil can be determined only according to the feelings of pleasure and pain. We can therefore neither give an accurate, objective standard nor explain the imperative elements of moral goodness. Moreover, to regard pleasure as the sole objective of life does not truly accord with the facts of actual human life. We can in no way be satisfied by pleasure. Anyone who takes only pleasure as the goal of life acts against human nature.

CHAPTER 23

The Good (Energetism)

I have discussed several views of the good and pointed out their insuf-
ficiencies, so I believe that what is entailed in the true understanding of
the good has become more clear. Let us now consider the good that
must be the goal of our will, that is, the standard that must determine
the value of our conduct. As I said before, we must seek the basis of
value judgments in direct experience found in our consciousness. The
good must be articulated from the internal demands of consciousness,
not from without. We cannot explain how a thing ought to be simply
from how it is or how it occurred. The ultimate standard of truth is
found in the internal necessity of consciousness. Foundational thinkers

such as Augustine and Descartes started from this point, and we, too, must seek the fundamental standard of good therein.

Heteronomous ethics locates the standard of good and evil as outside us; taking that perspective, such ethics cannot explain why we ought to do the good. In comparison, the approach taken by the rational theory, in which the value of good and evil is determined from reason as one of the internal activities of consciousness, is a step forward—but even so, reason cannot determine the value of the will. As Høffding[1] has indicated in his claim that consciousness begins and ends with the action of the will, the will is a more fundamental fact than the activity of abstract understanding—it is not that the activity of abstract understanding gives rise to the will, but that the will controls this activity. It might be acceptable for hedonic theories to state that feeling and the will are probably manifestations of the same phenomenon with differing strengths, but as seen before, pleasure arises from the satisfaction of the innate demands of consciousness, and such innate demands as impulses and instincts are more fundamental than feelings of pleasure and discomfort.

To explain the good it is clear that we must investigate the character of the will. The will is the fundamental unifying activity of consciousness and a direct manifestation of the fundamental unifying power of reality. The will entails action for oneself, not for the sake of another. The basis for the determination of the value of the will can be sought only in the will itself. As stated in the discussion of the nature of conduct, the action of the will has the following character: at the base of the will are innate demands (the causes of consciousness) that appear in consciousness as goal concepts which unify consciousness; when such unification reaches completion—when ideals are realized—we feel satisfaction. When we go against these ideals, we feel dissatisfaction. Because that which determines the value of conduct lies wholly in these fundamental, innate demands of the will, when we completely realize these demands (our ideals), our conduct is praised as good, and when we act contrary to them, our conduct is censured as bad. Accordingly, the good is the realization of our internal demands, our ideals; it is the development and completion of the will.

The ethical theory that bases itself on such fundamental ideals is called

---

1. Harald Høffding (1843–1931), a Danish philosopher and historian of philosophy, takes will in a broad sense to be more fundamental than knowledge and feeling.

energetism, and its origin is found in Plato and Aristotle. Aristotle wrote that the goal of human life is happiness (*eudaimonia*), and that we reach this happiness through perfect action, not through the pursuit of pleasure.

Many so-called moralists overlook this aspect of action. Focusing on duty and laws, they believe that the fundamental nature of the good is to suppress the desires of the self and to restrict action. Lacking an understanding of the true significance of our actions, we imperfect beings of course often fall into predicaments—so it is only natural that people should talk of suppressing desires and restricting action. But it is only because there is a greater demand to be fostered that we need to suppress smaller demands; therefore to suppress all demands indiscriminately in fact runs contrary to the fundamental nature of the good. The good must include a quality of imperative authority, but natural enjoyment is a more necessary quality. There is no inherent value in moral duty and moral law itself, for they arise on the basis of the great demands discussed earlier.

From this perspective, the good and happiness do not conflict, and like Aristotle we can say that the good is happiness. The satisfaction of the demands of the self or the realization of ideals always constitutes happiness. Although this feeling of happiness necessarily accompanies the good, we cannot maintain—as hedonic theories do—that the feeling of pleasure is the goal of the will and that pleasure is the good. Although they resemble each other, pleasure and happiness are different. We can achieve happiness through satisfaction, and satisfaction arises in the realization of demands for ideals. "Eating coarse food, drinking water, and bending one's elbow to make a pillow—pleasure also resides therein," said Confucius.[2] Depending on the circumstances, we are able to maintain happiness even in the midst of pain. True happiness is actually something acquired through the realization of ideals. People of course often view the realization of the ideals of the self or the satisfaction of demands as identical with egoism and selfishness; but for us the voice of the deepest internal demands of the self has great power, and there is nothing in human nature more awe-inspiring than this.

2. This statement by Confucius is found in book 7 of the *Analects*. Arthur Waley offers this translation: "He who seeks only coarse food to eat, water to drink and bent arm for pillow, will without looking for it find happiness to boot." Arthur Waley, trans., *The Analects of Confucius* (New York: Vintage, n.d.), 126.

Assuming that the good is the realization of ideals and the satisfaction of demands, from what do these demands or ideals arise and what sort of character does the good have? Because the will is the deepest unifying activity in consciousness—that is, the action of the self—the fundamental demands or ideals that become the cause of the will arise from the character of the self and are the power of the self. In our consciousness, an internal unity always functions at the base of thinking, imagination, will, perception, feeling, and impulse; and all phenomena of consciousness are the development and completion of this unity. The deepest power unifying this whole is our so-called self, and the will is that which most completely expresses this power. Thus the development and completion of the will is none other than the development and completion of the self, and the good is the development and completion—the self-realization—of the self. The highest good, in other words, is for our spirit to develop its various abilities and to achieve a perfect development. In this way, Aristotle's *entelechie* is the good.[3] For a human to display his or her innate nature—just as a bamboo plant or a pine tree fully displays its nature—is our good. Spinoza said that virtue is to function in accordance with the self 's own nature.[4]

From this perspective, the concept of good approaches that of beauty. Beauty is felt when things are realized like ideals are realized, which means for things to display their original nature. Just as flowers are most beautiful when they manifest their original nature, humans attain the pinnacle of beauty when they express their original nature. In this regard the good is beauty. No matter how valueless conduct might appear when seen in light of the great demands of human nature, when it is truly natural conduct emerging from the innate talents of the person, it evokes a sense of beauty. In the moral realm this conduct likewise gives rise to a kind of magnanimous feeling. The Greeks regarded the good and beauty as identical, an idea most evident in Plato.

Moreover, from a certain angle, the concept of the good coincides

---

3. *Entelechie* is both the completed reality of an entity and the power of the entity to reach completion.

4. In his *Ethics* Spinoza writes that "true virtue is nothing else but living in accordance with reason; while infirmity is nothing else but man's allowing himself to be led by things which are external to himself, and to be by them determined to act in a manner demanded by the general disposition of things rather than by his own nature considered solely in itself." Dagobert D. Runes, ed., *The Ethics of Spinoza: The Road to Inner Freedom* (Secaucus, N.J.: Citadel Press, 1976), 100.

with the concept of reality. As discussed earlier, the development and completion of a thing is the fundamental mode of the establishment of all reality, and spirit, nature, and the universe come to exist by this mode. The good, conceived of as the development and completion of the self, amounts to our obeying the laws of the reality called the self. That is, to unite with the true reality of the self is the highest good. The laws of morality thus come to be included in the laws of reality, and we are able to explain the good in terms of the true nature of the reality called the self. Internal demands, which are the basis of value judgments, and the unifying power of reality are one, not two. The view of existence and value as separate comes from an act of abstraction that distinguishes objects of knowing from objects of feeling and willing; but in concrete reality existence and value are fundamentally one. Thus, to seek the good and to return to it is to know the true reality of the self. The notion of the truth and the good as being identical in the rational theory is partially true, but abstract knowledge and the good do not necessarily coincide. To know the true reality of the self means to have an existential realization.

The above ideas are fundamental to Plato's stance (that the idea of the good is the foundation of reality) in Greece and to the *Upanishads* in India. And in medieval philosophy we encounter the expression, "All reality is good" (*omne ens est bonum*). I think such ideas constitute the most profound notion of the good.

The Good as a Unity
of Personality

Having set forth a general conception of the good, I will henceforth examine the good in greater detail and clarify its distinctive characteristics.

All of us clearly recognize that consciousness is not a simple activity but rather a synthesis of various activities. The demands that arise in us are not simple either, but are quite naturally varied. This brings us to a question, which concerns the good of the self as a whole: the fulfillment of which demand constitutes the highest good?

None of our phenomena of consciousness stands alone; without exception each comes forth in relation to others. A moment of consciousness is not simple—it contains complex elements that are dependent on each other, for they have a kind of meaning in relation to others. Consciousness at a given time and also over a lifetime is organized into such a system, and the "self " is the name for the unity of this whole.

Our demands likewise never arise alone. They also necessarily arise in relation to others. The good for us differs from the satisfaction of just one kind of demand or a demand of a particular time. Clearly, a particular demand becomes good only when it is related to the whole. For example, the good of the body derives not from the health of one of its parts but from the harmony of the body as a whole. From the perspective of energetism, then, the good is primarily a coordinated harmony—or mean—between various activities. Our conscience is the activity of consciousness that harmonizes and unifies the activities.

The idea that harmony constitutes the good comes from Plato. He likens the good to harmony in music, and such people as Shaftesbury[1] have adopted this idea. Aristotle theorizes that the mean is the good, and the Asian version of this idea appears in *The Book of the Mean*.[2] Aristotle locates all virtues in the mean, contending for example that courage is the mean between roughness and timidity, and that frugality is the mean between miserliness and squander, a view that closely resembles the thought of Tzu-ssu.[3] On the basis of the theory of evolution Herbert Spencer[4] similarly contends that the good is the average of various faculties, which amounts to the same view as the others just mentioned.

Simply saying that the good is a harmony or the mean, however, does not sufficiently clarify its meaning. What meaning do harmony and the mean have here? Consciousness is not an assemblage of sequential actions

1. Anthony Ashley Cooper Shaftesbury, the Earl of Shaftesbury (1671–1713), worked in the areas of aesthetics and moral philosophy. He believed in the possibility of a harmony, based on innate human predispositions, between the individual and society, and between egoism and altruism. He regarded beauty as a kind of harmony, found especially in music. His main work was *Characteristiks of Men, Manners, Opinions, Time* (1711).

2. Along with Confucius's *Analects*, *The Book of Mencius*, and the *Great Learning*, *The Book of the Mean* is one of the "Four Books" in classical Chinese thought. It was originally one chapter in the *Li Chi*, or record of rites, which is one of the "Five Classics."

3. A grandson of Confucius, Tzu-ssu is traditionally considered the author of the *Li Chi* and hence of *The Book of the Mean* as well.

4. Herbert Spencer (1820–1903) elaborated on Darwin's notion of evolution, especially in terms of increasing heterogeneity. Based on evolutionary thought, his ethical theory is utilitarian, identifying ethical values or the good as being that which is conducive to long-term pleasure. He set forth such ideas in *First Principles* (1862) and *Principles of Ethics* (2 vols., 1879–93).

but a single unified system. Accordingly, harmony or the mean does not carry a quantitative connotation; it must signify a systematic order. Granting this, what is the order that is distinct in each of the various activities of our spirit? At lower levels, our spirit, like the spirit of animals, is simply an instinctual activity—that is, because it functions impulsively in response to objects before us, it is moved entirely by physical desire. But no matter how simple, phenomena of consciousness necessarily possess ideational demands; however instinctual the activity of consciousness might be, the activity of ideas is hidden behind it. (I think that this is necessarily the case with higher non-human animals as well.) With the possible exception of the severely retarded, no humans can be satisfied by purely physical desires, for ideational desires are always functioning at the bottom of their minds. In short, all people embrace some sort of ideals. Even a miser's craving for profit derives from a kind of ideal. Human beings do not exist on the basis of the flesh—rather, they live on the basis of ideas. In his poem "The Violet," Goethe writes that a violet in the field achieves the fulfillment of love when it is crushed under the foot of a young shepherdess.[5] I take this to be the true feeling of all humans.

The activity of ideas is the fundamental activity of spirit, and by this our consciousness should be controlled. The true good for us is to satisfy the demands arising from that activity. Granting this and proceeding a step farther to inquire into the fundamental law of the activity of ideas, we come to the laws of reason. The laws of reason express the most universal and fundamental relations between ideas; they are supreme laws controlling the activity of ideas. Reason is the basic faculty that should control our spirit, and the satisfaction of reason is our highest good. It can thus be said that human good is to follow reason. Rigorously emphasizing this idea, the Cynics and Stoics rejected all other desires of the human mind as evil and even argued that the sole good is to follow reason alone. In the later thought of Plato and Aristotle, however, the highest good derives from the activity of reason, and to control and govern other activities by it constitutes the good as well. In the *Republic,*

5. In the poem Goethe depicts a violet's love for a youthful shepherdess—the violet longs to catch her eye and to be held by her: "Alas! Alas! the maid drew nigh, / The violet failed to meet her eye, / She crushed the violet sweet. / It sank and died, yet murmured not: / "And if I die, oh, happy lot, / For her I die, / And at her happy feet!" John Storer Cobb, trans., and Nathan Haskell Dole, ed., *Goethe: Poetical Works, Reynard the Fox* (Boston: Dana Estes, 1902), 120.

Plato sees a parallel between the organization of the republic and that of the human soul and argues that the state of affairs governed by reason is the highest good for both the republic and the individual.

Assuming that our consciousness is constituted by a synthesis of various faculties and constructed such that one faculty controls the others, then in energetism to follow reason and on that basis control other faculties is the good. Originally, however, our consciousness is one activity, and a single, unique power always functions at its base. This power manifests itself in such momentary activities of consciousness as perception and impulse; in conscious activities like thinking, imagining, and willing, it assumes a more profound form. To follow reason means to follow this profound unifying power. Otherwise, as I stated when I critiqued the rational theory of ethics, reason conceived of in the abstract provides merely a formal relationship with no content whatsoever. The unifying power of consciousness never exists apart from the content of consciousness; in fact, the content of consciousness is established by this power. When we investigate the content of consciousness by analyzing it into its individual parts, we of course fail to discover this unifying power. It nevertheless appears as a majestic, indisputable fact in the synthesis of the individual parts. For example, an ideal expressed in a painting or a feeling expressed in music is understood not through analysis, but must be intuited and realized in oneself. If we regard this unifying power as the personality of each individual, then the good resides in the maintenance and development of personality as this unifying power.

The "power of personality" does not indicate a natural, material force as in the life-force of plants and animals, nor does it indicate such an unconscious faculty as instinct. Instinctual activity is a kind of material force that originates in organic activities. In contrast, personality is the unifying power of consciousness. Although I speak of it in this way, personality is not an assortment of highly subjective hopes that functions as the center of each person's superficial consciousness. Such hopes may express the individual's personality to some extent, but the true personality comes forth when a person eradicates them and forgets his or her self. But this is not the activity of Kant's pure reason, which is common to each individual and totally separate from the content of experience. Rather, personality must be something with a particular meaning unique to the person.

The true unity of consciousness is a pure and simple activity that comes forth of itself, unhindered by oneself; it is the original state of independent, self-sufficient consciousness, with no distinction among knowledge, feeling, and volition, and no separation of subject and object. At this time our true personality expresses itself in its entirety. Personality therefore is not found in mere reason or desire, much less in unconscious impulses; like the inspiration of a genius, it is an infinite unifying power that functions directly and spontaneously from within each individual. (People long ago said that the Way does not pertain to knowing or to not knowing.[6]) And as I discussed in the section on reality, if we assume that phenomena of consciousness are the only reality, then our personalities are the activity of the unifying power of the universe. In other words, our personalities are the particular forms in which the sole reality—which transcends the distinction between mind and matter—manifests itself according to circumstances.

Since the good is the realization of this great power, its demands are exceedingly solemn. Kant stated that there are two things that we always view with praise and reverence: the vast, starry heaven above, and the moral law within.[7]

6. In the *Mumonkan* (Ch. *Wu-men Kuan*), case nineteen, "Ordinary Mind is Tao," Nan Ch'uan states, "Tao does not belong to knowing or to not-knowing. Knowing is illusion; not-knowing is blankness." Zenkei Shibayama, *Zen Comments on the Mumonkan* (New York: Harper and Row, 1974), 140.

7. Kant makes this statement in his *Critique of Practical Reason*. He writes, "Two things fill the mind with ever new and increasing admiration and awe, the oftener and more steadily we reflect on them: the starry heavens above me and the moral law within me." Lewis White Beck, trans., *Critique of Practical Reason* (Indianapolis: Bobbs-Merrill, 1956), 166.

CHAPTER 25

The Motivation of Good Conduct (The Form of the Good)

As I stated earlier, the good refers to that which satisfies the internal demands of the self. Because the greatest demands of the self—that is, the demands of personality—are the fundamental unifying power of consciousness, to satisfy these demands and thereby actualize personality is for us the absolute good. The demands of the personality are the unifying power of consciousness and, at the same time, an expression of the infinite unifying power at the base of reality; and so to actualize and fulfill our personality means to become one with this underlying power. If we construe the good in this way, we can determine the nature of good conduct.

From this perspective, all good conduct takes personality as its goal.

Personality is the basis of all value, and in the universe only personality possesses absolute value. Within us are, of course, various demands, both physical and mental; therefore various things, such as wealth, power, knowledge, and art, are valuable to us. Yet no matter how powerful or lofty the demand, if it becomes divorced from the demands of personality it loses all value. A demand possesses value only as a part of, or a means of, the demands of personality. Wealth, honor, authority, health, skill, and academic knowledge are not in themselves good. When they run contrary to the demands of personality, they become evil. In short, absolutely good conduct is conduct that takes the actualization of personality as its goal, that is, conduct that functions for the sake of the unity of consciousness.

According to Kant, the value of things is determined from without and is thus relative, but because our will determines its value by itself, personality possesses absolute value. As is widely known, Kant taught that we should respect the personality of ourselves and others and treat others as ends in themselves, never using them merely as a means.

What sort of conduct is the good conduct that truly takes personality as its goal? To answer this question, we must consider the objective content of the action of personality and clarify the goal of conduct—but I will first discuss the subjective element in good conduct: the motivation. Good conduct is conduct that derives from the internal necessity of the self. We can be aware of the demands of the whole personality only in the state of direct experience prior to deliberative discrimination. In this state, personality is the voice of a type of internal demand that emerges from the depths of the mind and that gradually envelops the mind as a whole. Conduct that takes personality itself as its goal is conduct that accords with this demand. If we go against it, we negate our own personality. Another condition necessary for good conduct is sincerity. Christ said that only those who are like an innocent child can enter heaven. Sincerity is the good not because of the results arising from it, but because it is good in itself. It is said that to deceive a person is evil, not necessarily because of what results from deceiving someone but rather because to deceive another is to deceive oneself and to negate one's own personality.

Such expressions as "the internal necessity of the self " and "genuine, unaffected demands" are occasionally misunderstood. Some people think that genuine unaffectedness lies in self-indulgently and recklessly overlooking the rules of society and in not restraining one's sensual desires.

But the internal necessity of personality—that is, sincerity—is a demand based on the union of knowledge, feeling, and volition. It does not indicate simply following blind impulse in opposition to judgments made by the intellect and the demands of human feeling. It is only when we exhaust the intellect and feeling that the true demand of personality—sincerity—arises in us; it is only when we exhaust all of the power of the self, when the consciousness of the self nearly disappears and one is not conscious of the self, that we see the activity of the true personality. Take, for example, a work of art. When does the true personality or originality of the painter appear? Insofar as the painter intends various things in his or her consciousness, we cannot yet truly see the painter's personality. We first see it only when, after long years of struggle, the painter's skills mature and the brush follows the will. The expression of personality in the moral realm is no different from this. We express personality not by following temporary desires but by following the most solemn internal demands. This is diametrically opposed to self-indulgent decadence and, contrary to what one might expect, it is an endeavor of difficulty and pain.

To follow the sincere internal demands of the self—to actualize the true personality of the self—does not mean to establish subjectivity in opposition to objectivity or to make external objects obey the self. Only when we thoroughly eliminate the subjective fancies of the self and unite with a thing can we satisfy the true demands of the self and see the true self. From a certain angle, the objective world of each individual is a reflection of his or her personality. Or rather, each individual's true self is the system of independent, self-sufficient reality appearing before that person. In this way, the sincerest demands of each and every person necessarily coincide at all times with the ideals of the objective world the person sees. For example, however selfish one might be, if one has any degree of sympathy, the greatest demand is certainly to give satisfaction to others after securing one's own satisfaction. If we assume that the demands of the self are not limited to carnal desires but include idealistic demands, then we must by all means speak in this way. The more selfish we become, the more we feel anguish at blocking the personal desires of others. Contrary to what one might think, I believe that perhaps only someone devoid of personal desire can obliterate the personal desires of others without losing peace of mind. To fulfill the greatest demands of the self and to actualize the self is to actualize the objective ideals of the self—that is, to unite with objectivity. In this regard, good conduct is love. Love is the feeling of congruence between self and other, the feeling of the union of subject and object. Love exists not only when one person faces another, but also when a painter encounters nature. In his renowned *Symposium,* Plato states that love is the feeling that arises when that which is lacking tries to return to its original, perfect state.

If we go a step farther, however, we find that truly good conduct is neither to make objectivity follow subjectivity nor to make subjectivity follow objectivity. We reach the quintessence of good conduct only when subject and object merge, self and things forget each other, and all that exists is the activity of the sole reality of the universe. At that point we can say that things move the self or that the self moves things, that Sesshū[1] painted nature or that nature painted itself through Sesshū. There is no fundamental distinction between things and the self, for just as the objective world is a reflection of the self, so is the self a reflection of the objective world. The self does not exist apart from the world that it sees. Heaven and earth grow from the same root, and the myriad things are one system. Sages in ancient India said, *"Tat twam asi"* (That thou art); Paul said, "It is no longer I who live, but Christ who lives in me" (Galatians 2:20); and Confucius said, "I follow what my heart desires, without overstepping the bounds of morality."[2]

---

1. Sesshū (1420–1506) is considered one of the greatest painters in Japanese history. He went to China in 1463 and returned six years later with Chinese styles that had a great impact on Japanese landscape painting.

2. This is an English translation of Nishida's Japanese rendering of Confucius's statement in the *Analects*: "[At seventy] I could follow the dictates of my own heart; for what I desired no longer overstepped the boundaries of right." Waley, *The Analects of Confucius,* 88.

CHAPTER 26

The Goal of Good Conduct (The Content of the Good)

In explaining good conduct that takes human personality as its goal, I indicated the kind of motives from which good conduct must emerge; I will now discuss the goal of good conduct. Good conduct is not a mere event inside consciousness but rather an action that takes as its goal the creation of an objective result in this world of facts, and we must now clarify the concrete content of this goal. I discussed earlier the so-called form of the good, and now I will discuss the content of the good.

Personality, which is both the unifying power of consciousness and the unifying power of reality, is first actualized in individuals. At the base of one's consciousness exists unanalyzable individuality. All activities of consciousness are an expression of this individuality: each person's knowledge, feeling, and volition possess qualities unique to the person. This individuality does not manifest itself only in phenomena of consciousness; it also emerges in each person's appearance, speech, and behavior. Without doubt, it is this individuality that portraits are meant to express. It starts to act at the moment a person is born into this world, and it develops in accordance with various experiences and circumstances until the time of death. Scientists reduce this individuality to the constitution of the brain, but I consider it an expression of the infinite unifying power of reality.

From the outset, we must make the actualization of this individuality our goal. This is the most immediate good. Health and knowledge are to be valued, of course, but they themselves are not the good, and we are not satisfied by them alone. That which gives an individual ultimate satisfaction is the actualization of the individuality of the self—that is, the displaying of one's own distinctive characteristics in practice. Anyone can give full play to individuality regardless of natural talents and life circumstances. Just as everyone has a different face, everyone possesses unique characteristics that cannot be imitated by others. The realization of this individuality gives supreme satisfaction to each person and makes each an indispensable part of the evolution of the universe. Until now, people have not emphasized individual good to any great extent, but I hold the good of the individual is most important and that it serves as the basis of all other goods. Truly great people are so not because of the greatness of their achievements, but because they have displayed great individuality. If one climbs to a high place and yells, one's voice will probably carry a long way because the place is high, not because the voice is loud. I believe that people who thoroughly express their own unique characteristics are greater than those who forget their duty to themselves and heedlessly run around for the sake of others.

This individual good differs from self-interest and selfish desires. Individualism and egoism must be strictly distinguished. Egoism is selfishness that takes one's own pleasure as its goal. This is the polar opposite of individualism, for to give full rein to the material desires of the self is, in fact, to eradicate individuality. No matter how many pigs we might gather together, none will have individuality.

Individualism and communalism are spoken of as if diametrically opposed to each other, but I think that they coincide. It is only when individuals in society fully engage in action and express their natural talents that society progresses. A society that ignores the individual is anything but a healthy one.

A strong will is the virtue most necessary for individual good. Such a person as Ibsen's character Brand[1] embodies the ideal of individual morality. In contrast, weakness of will and vanity are the most despicable evils (and both of them arise from the loss of self-esteem). The greatest crime against individuality occurs when people commit suicide in despair.

As said earlier, true individualism is never reproachable nor does it necessarily conflict with society. But are people's individualities independent, unrelated realities? Or are individuals all expressions of a social self that functions at our base? If the former is the case, then individual good must be our greatest good. If the latter is the case, then there is a greater social good in us. I think that Aristotle gets at an indisputable truth when he states at the beginning of his study of politics that people are social animals. Seen from the perspective of contemporary physiology, our physical bodies are not entirely individual, for they originate in the cells of our ancestors. We and our descendants are born through the splitting of these cells. We can thus view all members of each species as constituting one living entity. Biologists now state along these lines that in a sense a living thing does not die, and this is also the case with the life of consciousness. When humans live in communities, a social consciousness necessarily functions to unify the consciousness of the members.

Language, manners, customs, social systems, laws, religion, and literature are all phenomena of this social consciousness. Our individual consciousnesses emerge from and are nurtured by it, and they are single cells that constitute this great consciousness. Knowledge, morality, and aesthetic taste all have social significance, and even the most universal learning does not escape social convention. (It is for this reason that at present each nation has its own academic tradition.) The distinctive characteristics of an individual are simply variations that derive from the social consciousness at their base. Even the most original genius cannot step beyond the scope of this social consciousness; in fact, such a person is one who most displays the deepest significance of the social consciousness. (Christ's relationship to Judaism is one example of this.) In short,

---

1. Henrik Ibsen (1828–1906), a Norwegian poet and playwright, wrote the play *Brand* in 1866. It is about the protagonist Brand's tragic struggle for self-realization.

anyone who stands absolutely unrelated to the social consciousness has the consciousness of the insane.

No one can deny these facts, but we encounter conflicting opinions about whether communal consciousness exists in the same sense as individual consciousness and can therefore be seen as a single personality. Høffding and others deny the existence of a unified consciousness. Høffding states that a forest is a collection of trees and that if the forest were divided there would no longer be a forest; likewise, a society is a collection of individuals, and there is no independent existence called a society that stands apart from individuals.[2] We cannot say, however, that there is no unity simply because unity no longer exists after the dissection of the whole. If we analyze individual consciousness, we do not find a separate, unifying self. But because there is a unity upon which a unique character arises and various phenomena are established, we consider this unity a living reality. For the same reason, we can view social consciousness as a living reality. Like individual consciousness, social consciousness constitutes a system with a center and interconnections. Individual consciousness of course has a foundation called the body, and in this respect it diverges from social consciousness. But the brain is not a simple material object—it is a collection of cells. This is no different from the fact that society is made up of the cells called individuals.

Because our individual consciousnesses are parts of such a social consciousness, most of our demands are social. If we were to remove all altruistic elements from our desires almost nothing would remain. This is clear when we see our desire for life as caused primarily by altruism. We find greater overall satisfaction in the satisfaction experienced by what the self loves and by the society to which one belongs than in personal satisfaction. Fundamentally, the center of the self is not limited to the interior of the individual: the self of a mother is found in her child, and the self of a loyal subject is found in the monarch. As one's personality becomes greater, the demands of the self become increasingly social.

Such social consciousness consists of various levels. The smallest and most immediate is the family, which is the first level at which one's personality develops in society. The purpose of a man and a woman joining together and forming a family is not only to leave descendants, for it involves a more profound spiritual (and moral) goal. In the *Symposium*, Plato relates a story to the effect that although man and woman

2. Nishida's note is "Høffding, *Ethik*, S.157."

were originally of one body, Zeus splits them apart, leaving them in a state of yearning for each other. This is an intriguing idea. If we consider what an exemplar of humankind might be, we see that an individual man or woman falls short, whereas that which combines masculinity and femininity does not. Otto Weininger states that humans, in both mind and body, are constituted by the union of masculine and feminine elements, and that the sexes love each other so that these elements can join together and constitute a complete human being.[3] Just as a man's character falls short of the exemplar of humankind, so does a woman's. The sexes complement each other and can thereby bring about the development of a complete personality.

The development of social consciousness is not limited to the small group of the family. Our mental and physical life can develop in all of the various social groups. At the next level beyond the family, the nation unifies the entirety of our conscious activity and expresses a single personality. Many theories have been set forth concerning the goal of the nation. Some people consider the essence of the nation to be the power of sovereignty and think that the purpose of the nation is to ward off enemies on the outside and protect life and property of the people on the inside. (Schopenhauer, Taine,[4] and Hobbes hold this opinion.) Others consider the essence of the nation to be the individual, and see the harmonious development of individual personalities as constituting its purpose. (This is the type of theory advanced by such people as Rousseau.)[5] But the true goal of the nation is not something material and passive as outlined by the former group, and the personality of an individual is not the foundation of the nation as maintained by the latter. We individuals are entities that have developed as cells of one society. The essence of the nation is the expression of the communal consciousness that constitutes the foundation of our minds. In the context of the nation, we can accomplish a great development of personality; the nation is a unified personality, and the systems and laws of the nation are expressions of the will of this communal consciousness. (This theory was set forth in antiquity by Plato and Aristotle and in modern times by Hegel.) To exert ourselves for the sake of a nation is to exert ourselves for the

3. Otto Weininger (1880–1903), a German psychologist, wrote about the human personality and sex differences in *Sex and Character* (*Geschlect und Charakter*).

4. Hippolyte Taine (1828–1893) was a French philosopher, historian, and critic.

5. Jean-Jacques Rousseau (1712–1778) argues in the *Social Contract* that the common good ultimately supports the individual's good.

sake of the development and perfection of a great personality. Moreover, when a nation punishes an individual, it does so neither for revenge nor for the safety of society, but because personality possesses an inviolable dignity.

At present, the nation is the greatest expression of unified communal consciousness. But the expression of our personality cannot stop there— it demands something greater: a social union that includes all human- kind. This idea has already appeared in Paul's Christianity and in the thought of the Stoics, but it is not easily actualized. The present age is still one of armed peace.

If we retrace the development of humankind from the beginning of history, we see that the nation is not the final goal of humankind. A meaningful purpose runs consistently throughout the development of humankind, and the nation appears to be something that rises and falls in order to fulfill part of humankind's mission. (The history of nations is the development of Hegel's so-called "world spirit.") Genuine univer- salism, however, does not require that each nation ceases to be. Rather, it means that each nation becomes increasingly stable, displays its dis- tinctive characteristics, and contributes to the history of the world.

CHAPTER 27

Perfect Good Conduct

The good is the actualization[1] of personality. Viewed internally, this actualization is the satisfaction of a solemn demand—that is, the unification of consciousness—and its ultimate form is achieved in the mutual forgetting of self and other and the merging of subject and object. Viewed externally as an emergent fact, this actualization advances from the small-scale development of individuality to a culmination in the large-scale unified development of all humankind. In considering these internal and external views of the actualization of personality, we must resolve a key

---

1. The Japanese term *jitsugen* can be rendered "actualization," "realization," or "fulfillment."

problem: can we deem that which gives us great satisfaction internally to be a great good in the realm of external facts as well? This is the problem of whether these two facets of the good are always congruent.

Based on my discussion of reality, I hold that these two facets in no way conflict with or contradict each other. Phenomena fundamentally involve no distinction between internal and external. Subjective consciousness and the objective world are the same thing viewed from different angles, so concretely there is only one fact. As stated before, the world is established by the self's unity of consciousness, and the self is one small system of reality. As emphasized in basic Buddhist thought, the self and the universe share the same foundation; or rather, they are the same thing. For this reason we can feel in our minds the infinite significance of reality as infinite truth in knowledge, as infinite beauty in feeling, and as infinite good in volition. To know reality is not to know something external to the self but to know the self itself. The truth, beauty, and good of reality are the truth, beauty, and good of the self. Doubts may arise as to why if this is so we encounter falsehood, ugliness, and evil in the world. When we consider this problem deeply, however, we see that in the world there is neither absolute truth, beauty, and good, nor absolute falsehood, ugliness, and evil. Falsehood, ugliness, and evil always arise in our viewing abstractly just one aspect of things while we are unaware of the whole, and in being partial to just one facet of reality and thereby going against the unity of the whole. (As I said in chapter nine, falsehood, ugliness, and evil are in one respect necessary for the establishment of reality; they are generated by a principle of opposition.)

According to Augustine, fundamentally no evil exists in the world and all of nature as created by God is good. Evil is merely the privation of essential qualities. God adorned the world with opposites as in a beautiful poem; and just as shadow increases a picture's beauty, the world is—when seen with insight—beautiful even while including sin.

In considering how the fact of the good and the demands of the good might conflict, we discover two cases. One is when a certain conduct is good in actuality but its motive is not good, and the other is when the motive is good but the conduct is not. In the first case, if an internal motive is selfish while the external conduct in actuality accords with a good goal, then the conduct falls short of good conduct that takes the actualization of personality as its goal. We might praise such conduct, but at such a time we are viewing it not in terms of morality but simply in terms of benefit. From the perspective of morality, this conduct is inferior to that of someone who, no matter how foolish he or she might be, has demonstrated the utmost sincerity. It might be said that conduct that tries to benefit many people—even if it does not spring from a purely good motive—is superior to the conduct of someone who tries to purify himself or herself. To benefit people can mean various things. If we are speaking of merely material benefit, the benefit will be good if it is used toward good ends but evil if it is used toward evil ends. Considered in light of the truly moral benefit that promotes so-called public morality, if conduct is not true good conduct internally, then it is merely a means to promote good conduct rather than good conduct itself. It does not measure up to instances of good conduct, no matter how minor they might be.

Regarding the second case—when the motive is good but the actual conduct is not necessarily good—people often say that individual sincerity and the supreme good of all humankind sometimes conflict. I believe, however, that those who say this lack a correct understanding of sincerity—what such people say is not true if we use "sincerity" in the sense of the truly deepest demands of spirit as a whole. Our true demands are not artificially created by us; they are facts of nature. Like truth or beauty at the base of the human mind, the good contains a universal element. Just as Faust discovered when he returned late at night to his lonely study after a walk in the fields during a time of great anguish over life, in the quiet of night when our minds are at peace the feeling of the universality of the good begins to operate in us spontaneously.[2] Assuming that no person possesses an entirely different basis of consciousness, I think that insofar as we are humans with shared reason we necessarily think in the same way and seek things in the same way. To be sure, there may be times when the greatest demands of humankind get stuck in mere possibility and do not actualize themselves and function. But even then it is not that there are no demands; the demands are hidden, and the self does not know the true self.

For this reason, I think that our deepest demands and greatest goals unite automatically. While internally we discipline the self and attain to the true nature of the self, externally we give rise to love for our fellow humans and come to accord with the supremely good goal—good conduct that is perfect and true. From one angle, such perfect good conduct appears exceedingly difficult, but from a different angle, it is something anyone must be able to do. Morality is not a matter of seeking something apart from the self—it is simply the discovery of something within the

2. Nishida's note is *"Goethe, Faust, Erster Teil Studierzimmer."*

self. People frequently confuse the essence of the good with its external shell, so they think that unless one is engaged in a worldwide enterprise involving all humankind, one stands unrelated to the greatest good. But because a person's abilities and circumstances determine what sort of enterprise will be undertaken, it is impossible for all people to pursue the same enterprise. Yet no matter how much our enterprises differ, we can function with the same spirit. No matter how small the enterprise, a person who constantly works out of love for his or her fellow humans realizes the great personality of all humankind. Although Raphael's lofty aesthetic personality perhaps found the Madonna the most appropriate medium for its realization, his personality manifests itself not only in the Madonna but in all of his paintings.[3] And though the subjects chosen by Raphael and Michelangelo are quite similar, the two artists express their respective characters in their own distinctive ways. In short, the essence of art and morality lies in spirit, not in things of the external world.

In closing this chapter, I want to say one more thing. When we approach the good academically, we can offer various explanations, but in actuality there is only one true good: to know the true self. Our true self is the ultimate reality of the universe, and if we know the true self we not only unite with the good of humankind in general but also fuse with the essence of the universe and unite with the will of God—and in this religion and morality are culminated. The method through which we can know the true self and fuse with God is our self-attainment of the power of the union of subject and object. To acquire this power is to kill our false self and, after dying once to worldly desire, to gain new life. (As Muhammad said, heaven lies in the shadow of the sword.) Only in this way can we truly reach the realm of the union of subject and object, which is the ultimate meaning of religion, morality, and art. Christianity calls this event rebirth, and Buddhism calls it *kenshō*.[4] According to one story, when Pope Benedict XI asked Giotto[5] to show him a work that demonstrated his ability as a painter, Giotto simply drew a circle. In morality, we must attain to Giotto's circle.

3. A key figure in the Renaissance, Raphael (1483–1520) painted many Madonnas, the most famous of which are the Madonna del Cardellino (1506), the Belle Jardinière (1507), and the Sistine Madonna (1518). William Rose Benét, *The Reader's Encyclopedia* (hereafter *RE*), 2d ed. (New York: Thomas Y. Crowell, 1985), 842.

4. *Kenshō* literally means to "see (into) one's Nature," and it is virtually synonymous with another Zen term, *satori*, awakening.

5. Giotto di Bondone (1266–1337) was a pre-Renaissance Florentine painter who parted from the Byzantine tradition. Benét, *RE*, 398.

PART IV

Religion

CHAPTER 28

The Religious Demand

The religious demand concerns the self as a whole, the life of the self. It is a demand in which the self, while perceiving its relativity and finitude, yearns to attain eternal, true life by uniting with an absolutely infinite power. Paul expressed it when he wrote, "It is no longer I who live, but Christ who lives in me."[1] This is feeling all one's corporeal life nailed to the cross and then trying to live solely in accordance with God. True religion seeks the transformation of the self and the reformation of life. Christ said, "He who does not take his cross and follow me is not worthy

1. Galatians 2:20.

of me,"[2] and as long as one has even the slightest belief in the finite self, one has yet to acquire a true religious spirit.

Needless to say, the practices of praying to God for benefit in this world and continually reciting the name of Amida Buddha (*nenbutsu*) in order to gain rebirth in the Pure Land also diverge from a true religious spirit. Shinran is quoted in the *Tannishō*:[3] "The *nenbutsu* chanted in the heart to increase works leading to rebirth in the pure land is a practice based on one's own efforts." In the Christian tradition, relying on God's help or fearing God's punishment falls short of true Christianity and such approaches to religion are merely varieties of selfishness. Moreover, many people nowadays understand religion as existing for the sake of spiritual peace, and I regard even this view as mistaken. Such people believe that they have realized the true meaning of religion by ridding themselves of any active temperament and leading a passive life with little passion and anguish. But religion is not to be sought for the sake of spiritual peace—such peace is simply a by-product of religion. The religious demand is a great and unavoidable demand; it is a solemn demand of the will. Religion is a human being's goal, not a means to something else.

If we follow the lead of voluntarist psychologists and suppose that the will is the fundamental activity of the mind and that all mental phenomena assume the form of the will, then the mind or spirit is a system of demands. The most powerful demand, which constitutes the center of this system, is the self. To unify everything from that center over time—that is, to maintain and develop the self—constitutes our mental or spiritual life. As long as this unity advances we are alive, but if and when this unity falls apart we are all but dead mentally, though we may be physically alive.

Are we able, then, to unify everything around individual demands? That is, can an individual life be maintained and developed without limit? The world is not created for the individual, and individual demands are not the greatest demands of human existence. Individual life inevitably conflicts with the outside world; in the inner world it inevitably falls into contradiction. So we must seek an even greater life, an even greater unity,

2. Matthew 10:38.

3. The *Tannishō* (Statements Deploring Deviations from Faith) is a collection of talks by Shinran (1173–1262), founder of the Pure Land of Buddhism. The talks were compiled by his disciple, Yuien. See *Tannishō: A Primer*, trans. Dennis Hirota (Kyoto: Ryukoku University, 1982).

through a shift in the center of consciousness. This demand for a greater unity is discernable in the arising of our communal spirit, although its ultimate state is the religious demand. As long as we set up a subjective self in opposition to the objective world and try to unify that world by means of it, then no matter how great this self becomes, the unity will remain inescapably relative. An absolute unity is gained only by discarding the subjective unity and merging with an objective unity.

The unity of consciousness is necessary for the establishment of consciousness and also its fundamental demand. A consciousness without a unity is no different than nothingness. Consciousness is established through conflicts in its content, and the more diversified the content becomes, the more consciousness requires a greater unity. The greatest extent of this unity is our so-called objective reality, and this unity is culminated in the union of subject and object. Objective reality does not exist apart from subjective consciousness for it is the culmination of the unification of consciousness, which cannot be doubted and beyond which nothing can be sought. This culmination of the unity of consciousness— that is, the state of the union of subject and object—is not only the fundamental demand of consciousness but also the original state of consciousness. As Condillac said, when we first see light, it is not so much that we see it, but rather that we are the light itself.[4] For an infant, all initial sensations are directly the universe itself. In such a state, subject and object are not yet divided; the self and things are one reality—there is just one fact. Because the self and things are one, there is no truth to be sought and no desire to be satisfied. People exist together with God, and this is what is referred to as the Garden of Eden. As consciousness differentiates and develops, subject and object oppose each other and the self and other things go against each other. In this process, life brings us demands and anguish; we are separated from God, and the Garden is forever closed to Adam's descendants. But no matter how far consciousness differentiates and develops, it cannot separate from the unity seen in the union of subject and object; in our knowledge and volition we are always seeking this unity. The differentiation and development of consciousness is the other side of unity, and it is necessary for the establishment of consciousness. In fact, it constitutes a search for a greater

4. Etienne Condillac (1715–1780), an Encyclopedist, addressed epistemological issues in such works as *Essays on the Origin of Human Understanding* (1746) and *Treatise on Sensations* (1754).

unity, which is the alpha and omega of consciousness. Thus in this sense the religious demand is the demand for the unity of consciousness and, further, the demand for union with the universe.

The religious demand is the deepest and greatest demand of the human mind. We have various physical and mental demands, but they arise merely from single parts of the self—only religion constitutes a solution of the self as a whole. We may seek the unity of consciousness and the union of subject and object through knowledge and volition, but this results in an incomplete unity. Religion seeks the deepest unity behind knowledge and volition, the unity that is prior to the separation of the intellect and the will. All of our demands are differentiations that emerge from the religious demand, and their development results in a return to it. Contrary to what some might think, people were religious in the days before the human intellect blossomed. The pinnacle of learning and morality can in fact be reached only by entering the realm of religion.

People often ask why religion is necessary. This is identical to asking why we need to live. Religion does not exist apart from the life of the self, and the religious demand is the demand of life itself. Our questions about the necessity of religion reflect a lack of seriousness in our own life. Those who try to think seriously and to live seriously cannot help but feel an intense religious demand.

CHAPTER 29

The Essence of Religion

Religion is the relationship between God and human beings. We can think about God in various ways, but it is perhaps most appropriate to view God as the foundation of the universe; and by "human beings" I am referring to our individual consciousnesses. Various religions come into being in accordance with different ways of thinking about the relationship between God and humans. But what sort of relationship is the true religious relationship?

If we assume that the essences of God and humans differ fundamentally and that God is merely some sort of great power above and beyond us, then there is no true religious motive in our response to God. We might fear God and therefore follow God's commands, or we might curry favor with God and thereby seek happiness and benefit. These approaches are rooted in selfishness, and a mutual relationship between those with different natures cannot be established without an element of selfishness. William Robertson Smith[1] stated that religion does not emerge from fear of an unknowable power but from loving reverence for a God who has a blood relationship with oneself. Religion is not an individual's optional relation with a supernatural power, but a communal relationship between members of a society and the power that maintains the peace and order of the society. At the base of all religions must be a relationship between God and humans in which they share the same nature—that is, a relationship like that between father and child. But for God and the human to share the same losses and gains and for God to save and protect us is not yet true religion. God must be the foundation of the universe and our own foundation as well. To take refuge in God is to take refuge in that foundation. God must also be the goal of the myriad things in the universe and therefore the goal of humans as well. Each person finds in God his or her own true goal. Just as the hands and feet are parts of the human, the human is a part of God. Our taking refuge in God seems in a certain respect to be a loss of the self, but in another respect it is the way we find the self. Christ said, "He who finds his life shall lose it, and he who loses his life for my sake will find it,"[2] and this is the purest form of religion.

The relationship between God and the human in true religion must be of this sort. We pray and offer thanks to God not for the sake of the self's existence, but for our return to God as the source of the self—and we are grateful for our return to God. Moreover, God loves people not to give worldly happiness but to return them to God. God is the source of life, and we live only in God. In this respect alone is religion filled with life and does the feeling of true piety arise. If we merely resign and entrust ourselves to God, then we have yet to rid ourselves of the scent of the self and to realize the heart of true piety. That one finds the true self in God might be seen as emphasizing the self, but this is actually the reason for abandoning the self and praising God.

I think it is a fundamental idea of all religions that God and humans

1. William Robertson Smith (1846–1894) was a Scottish biblical scholar. His main works include *The Old Testament in the Jewish Church: A Course of Lectures in Biblical Criticism* (1881) and *Lectures on the Religion of the Semites: The Fundamental Institutions* (1889).

2. Matthew 10:39.

have the same nature, that in God humans return to their origin, and that only what is based on these two points can be called true religion. Beginning with this idea, however, we can conceptualize various kinds of relationships between God and humans. We can conceive of God as a transcendent entity apart from the universe who controls the world—including people—from the outside. Or we can think of God as immanent and functioning within people, who are all parts of God. The former is theism, the latter is pantheism. It might be rational to think along the lines of pantheism, but many religious figures oppose that view, for to see God and nature as identical is to eliminate God's personal character. When the myriad things in the universe are regarded as variant forms of God, not only is the transcendence of God lost and God's majesty marred, but the objectionable problem of having to attribute the origin of evil to God also arises. Thinking about this carefully, however, we see that pantheistic thought does not necessarily have such flaws and that theistic thought is not necessarily without them. If we view God and the essential nature of reality as identical while also viewing the foundation of reality as spiritual, then we will not necessarily lose God's personal character. Additionally, no form of pantheism holds that individual things are God just as they are. In Spinoza's philosophy, for example, the myriad things in this world are modes of God. Moreover, even in theism God's omniscience and omnipotence are not easily reconcilable with the existence of evil in the world; in fact, this problem plagued many medieval philosophers.

The idea of a transcendent God who controls the world from without not only conflicts with our reason but also falls short of the most profound religiosity. The only thing we can know to be the will of God is the laws of nature, and apart from these laws there is no divine revelation; of course, because God is unfathomable, what we know is perhaps only one part of God. Though we might assume a revelation apart from the laws of nature, we cannot know it; and if we assume that revelation opposes the laws of nature, then God involves a contradiction. People believe in the divinity of Jesus Christ because his life exhibits the deepest truth of human life. Our God must be the internal unifying power of the universe, which orders heaven and earth and nurtures the myriad things in them; apart from this power there is no God. If we say that God is personal, then at the base of reality we ascertain significance that involves personality. Otherwise, what we speak of as supernatural is either based on a historical legend or our own subjective fancy. It is moreover by directly seeing God at the base of nature and at the base of the self that we can feel God's infinite warmth and attain to the essence of religion, which is to live in God. The sense of true reverence and love for God can emerge only from living in God. Love means that two personalities have merged and become one, and reverence arises when a partial personality faces a perfect one. Reverence and love must be based on a unity of personality.

The feelings of love and reverence arise not only between people but also in one's own consciousness. Because our mutually divergent consciousness of today and yesterday possess the same center of consciousness, they are filled with feelings of self-reverence and self-love; likewise, the reason we revere and love God must be that we possess the same foundation as God and that our spirit is a part of God's consciousness. Even though God and humans have the same foundation of spirit, they can of course be regarded as independent in the same way that the minds of two people with the same thought are independent. This approach, however, makes temporal and spatial distinctions in spirit just as we do between physical bodies. In the case of spirit, whatever has the same foundation is the same spirit. We can view our consciousness, which changes from day to day, as always being the same spirit because it always possesses the same unity; in the same way, our spirit must be identical to God. The statement that we live in God is, then, not simply a metaphor but a fact. (In a commentary on John 17:21, even Bishop Wescott stated that the unity of believers is not merely a moral unity in terms of such factors as goal-emotion but a vital unity in the sense of life unity.)[3]

The most profound religion is thus established upon the unity of God and humans, and the true meaning of religion is found in grasping the significance of this unity, in breaking beyond one's own consciousness and experiencing the lofty universal spirit that functions at the base of consciousness. Faith should not be bestowed from without by a legend or theory—it should be cultivated from within. As Jakob Boehme said, we arrive at God through the deepest internal birth (*die innerste Geburt*). In this internal rebirth we see God directly and believe in God, and at the same time we find our true life and feel infinite power. Faith is not

3. Brooke Foss Wescott (1825–1901) was a Cambridge scholar and later an Anglican bishop who is widely known for the definitive version of the Greek New Testament that he edited with Fenton Hort (1828–1892). Williston Walker, Richard A. Norris, David W. Lotz, Robert Handy, *A History of the Christian Church*, 4th ed. (New York: Charles Scribner's Sons, 1985), 641.

mere knowledge, but an intuition and a vital force in the above sense. One unifying power functions at the base of all our mental activity, and we call it our self or personality. Subjective things such as desires as well as highly objective things such as knowledge take on the color of this unifying force, the personality of each person. Both knowledge and desire are established by this power.

Faith is thus a unifying power that transcends knowledge. It is not that faith is supported by knowledge and the will, but that knowledge and the will are supported by faith. In this sense, faith is mystical. But to say that faith is mystical does not mean that it is contrary to knowledge, for faith that conflicts with knowledge cannot become the basis of life. If we exhaust our intellect and will, then we will acquire from within a faith we cannot lose.

CHAPTER 30

God

God is the foundation of the universe. As said before, I do not regard God as a transcendent creator outside the universe, for God is the base of this reality. The relation between God and the universe is not like the relation between an artist and the artist's work; rather, it is the relation between a noumenon and a phenomenon. The universe is not a creation of God but a manifestation of God.[1] From the movement of the sun, moon, and stars without, to the intricate workings of the human mind within, there is nothing that is not a manifestation of God. We can worship the divine light of God in the foundation of each of these things.

1. In the original text Nishida inserted the English word "manifestation" for the accompanying Japanese term, *hyōgen*, which can also be rendered "expression."

Just as Newton and Kepler[2] were struck by a feeling of piety when they observed the order of the movement of heavenly bodies, so the more we study natural phenomena the surer we know that one unifying power in the background controls them. What people refer to as the advance of learning indicates the unity of this kind of knowledge. Hence, just as we recognize the control of one unifying power outside us in the foundation of nature, so too must we recognize the control of a unifying power within us at the base of the mind. Although the human mind assumes countless forms as if it follows no fixed law, upon contemplation it seems that a great unifying power controls it in all times and places. Taking this a step farther, we see that nature and spirit are not unconnected but, rather, closely interrelated. We cannot help thinking about the unity of the two—that is, there must be an even greater single unifying power at their base. All types of philosophy or science acknowledge this unity. And this unity is, namely, God. Of course, if materialists and scientists are correct in arguing that matter is the only reality and that all things simply follow the laws of material force, then we perhaps cannot conceive of such a thing as God. But is matter the true nature of reality?

As discussed before in regard to reality, we cannot know matter as an independent reality apart from our phenomena of consciousness. The given facts of direct experience are nothing other than our phenomena of consciousness, and what we call space, time, and material force are simply concepts established in order to organize these facts and to explain them. What physicists speak of as pure matter divorced from our individual nature is an abstract concept farthest removed from concrete facts. The closer we approach concrete facts, the more individual they become. The most concrete facts are most individual. Primitive explanations, as in myths, were therefore all anthropomorphic, but as pure knowledge advanced explanations became increasingly general and abstract and eventually generated such concepts as pure matter. Although such abstract explanations are exceedingly superficial and weak, we must not forget that our subjective unity lies behind them. The most fundamental explanation necessarily comes back to the self, for the self is the key to explaining the universe; therefore, to explain spirit according to matter is to invert the root and the branch.

2. Isaac Newton (1642–1727) and Johannes Kepler (1571–1630) established themselves as leading astronomers by setting forth, respectively, three laws of motion and three laws of planetary motion.

That which Newton and Kepler observed and took to be the order of natural phenomena is actually the order of our phenomena of consciousness. All consciousness is established according to a unity, which extends from the unity in the daily consciousness of each individual person to the universal unity of consciousness inclusive of all individual consciousnesses. (The idea that the unity of consciousness is limited to individual consciousness is a dogmatic assumption added on to pure experience.) The world of nature is a system of consciousness constituted by such a trans-individual unity. We unify the experience of the self by means of individual subjectivity and, further, unify the experience of all individuals by means of trans-individual subjectivity. The natural world arises as the object of this trans-individual subjectivity. Royce stated that our belief in the existence of nature is connected with our belief in the existence of our fellow humans.[3] The unity of the world of nature ultimately amounts to a kind of unity of consciousness.

Fundamentally, spirit and nature are not two separate kinds of reality; the distinction between them derives from different views of one and the same reality. In the facts of direct experience, there is no opposition between subject and object and no distinction between mind and matter; matter in itself is mind and mind in itself is matter, and there is only one actuality. The opposition of subject and object originates in conflicts of this system of reality, or—when seen from a certain angle—in the development of this system. In other words, in the continuation of perception there is no distinction between subject and object, for this opposition arises through reflection. When there is a conflict in the system of reality, the unifying activity is thought of as spirit and that which confronts it as its object is thought of as nature. In fact, however, objective nature cannot exist apart from a subjective unity, and we cannot expect to find a subjective unity without an object of unity, that is, content. Spirit and nature are the same kind of reality, differing only in terms of their forms of unity. Anything that leans toward one or the other is an abstract, incomplete reality. Reality first becomes a perfect, concrete reality in the union of the two. The unity of spirit and nature

3. Nishida's note is "Josiah Royce, *The World and the Individual,* Second Series, Lect. IV." Royce writes, "Our belief in the reality of Nature, when Nature is taken to mean the realm of physical phenomena known to common sense and to science, *is inseparably bound up with our belief in the existence of our fellow-men.*" Josiah Royce, *The World and the Individual* (New York: Macmillan, 1929), 165–66.

is not a unity of two types of systems—fundamentally they exist in one and the same unity.

If we assume that reality includes no distinction between spirit and nature; that there are not two types of unity; and that facts of direct experience lead to various discriminations depending on how we look at them, then God—the foundation of reality discussed before—must be the foundation of the facts of direct experience, the foundation of our phenomena of consciousness. Nevertheless, all of our phenomena of consciousness constitute a system. Even natural phenomena, which come to exist by virtue of a trans-individual unity, cannot separate from this mode. The self-development of a certain unifying entity is the mode of all realities, and God is their unifier. The relation between the universe and God is the relation between our phenomena of consciousness and their unity. Just as mental images in both thinking and willing are unified by a goal concept and as all things are expressions of this unifying concept, so is God the unifier of the universe and is the universe a manifestation of God. This comparison is not metaphorical—it is a fact. God is the greatest and final unifier of our consciousness; our consciousness is one part of God's consciousness and its unity comes from God's unity. In fact, all things—from such small-scale things as our joys and sorrows to such large-scale things as the movement of the sun, moon, and other heavenly bodies—are based on this unity. It was this great unity of universal consciousness that impressed Newton and Kepler.

What is the nature of God, who in this sense is both the unifier of the universe and the foundation of reality? That which governs spirit must be the laws of spirit. And as I said before, matter is nothing more than the shallowest of abstract concepts, established for the sake of explaining things. Mental phenomena are the activity of knowledge, feeling, and volition, and that which governs them must be their laws. But spirit is not a mere collection of these activities; a single unifying power underlies these phenomena, which are its expression. If we call this unifying power personality, then God is the great personality at the base of the universe. From natural phenomena to the historical development of humankind, there is nothing that does not assume the form of great thought and great will. The universe is an expression of God's personality.

Though I argue in this way, I do not agree with the thinkers in a certain school of thought who contend that God transcends the universe and, like our subjective spirit, has distinctive thought and will separate from the advance of the universe. In God, knowing is action and action is knowing. Reality is none other than the thought and will of God.[4] Such things as our subjective thinking and will are incomplete, abstract realities that arise from the conflict of various systems; we cannot attribute them to God. In *Personality, Human and Divine,* Illingworth sets forth self-consciousness, the freedom of the will, and love as elements of personality.[5] Before we take these three to be elements of personality, however, we must clarify what sort of actual facts these functions signify.

Self-consciousness is a phenomenon that accompanies the unification of a partial system of consciousness in the center of the entirety of consciousness. Self-consciousness arises through reflection, and the reflection of the self is the activity that in this way seeks the center of consciousness. The self is nothing other than the unifying activity of consciousness. If this unity changes, the self changes as well. To call anything else the essence of the self is to make an empty designation. Some people might think that if they reflect inwardly, they will then acquire a special kind of consciousness of the self, but such consciousness is, as psychologists point out, nothing more than a feeling that accompanies the unity. It is not that this unity arises because of such a consciousness, but that such consciousness arises because of the unity. The unity itself cannot become the object of knowledge; we can become it and function, but we cannot know it. True self-awareness exists upon the activity of the will, not upon intellectual reflection.

Construed in terms of the self-awareness in God's personality, each of the unities in the phenomena of the universe are none other than God's self-awareness. For example, the fact that the sum of the angles of a triangle is equal to the sum of two right angles is necessarily regarded in the same way by each person in each era. This, too, is one instance of the self-awareness of God. We perhaps can say that the notion of a universal unity that governs our spirit is a consciousness of God's self-

4. Nishida's note is "Spinoza, *Ethica,* I Pr. 17 Schol." In this proposition in his *Ethics* Spinoza states that "the intellect of God, in so far as it is conceived to constitute God's essence, is, in reality, the cause of things, both of their essence and their existence. This seems to have been recognized by those who have asserted that God's intellect, God's will, and God's power are one and the same." R. H. M. Elwes, trans., *The Chief Works of Benedict De Spinoza,* vol.2 (New York: Dover, 1951), 61–62.

5. John Richardson Illingworth (1848–1915) wrote on Christian ethics, God's immanence (*Divine Immanence: An Essay on the Spiritual Significance of Matter*), and reason and revelation.

identity. The myriad things in the world are established through God's unity, and in God, everything is an actuality. Further, God is always active. And in God there is no past or future—time and space arise by means of a universal unity of consciousness. In God, everything is the present. As Augustine said, because God created time and transcends it, God is in the eternal now. In God there is accordingly no reflection, memory, or hope, and hence no special self-consciousness. Because everything is the self and there is nothing apart from the self, there is no consciousness of the self.

The "freedom of the will" has various connotations as well. True freedom is the necessary freedom of functioning from the internal character of the self. A totally causeless will is not only something irrational but also a completely fortuitous event in the self and is not felt as constituting free conduct. As I have said, God is the basis of the countless beings in the universe, and no things exist apart from God. Because all things emerge from God's internal nature, God is free. In this sense God is absolute freedom. God might appear to be restricted by God's own nature and to lose omnipotence, but acting contrary to one's own nature indicates the imperfection of or the contradictions in one's nature. I do not think that God's perfection and omniscience can be established together with a variable free will. Augustine wrote that the will of God is unchanging; God does not sometimes desire certain things and then other times not desire them, much less cancel a previous decision.[6] Selective will must accompany the state of consciousness in us imperfect humans, and such willing ought not be attributed to God. With things we have fully mastered, for example, there is no room for selective will to enter; selective will becomes necessary in instances of doubt, contradiction, and conflict.

As all people say, knowledge of course includes freedom and signifies possibility. Possibility, however, does not have to signify a variable possibility. And knowledge is not limited to reflection, for intuition is a kind of knowledge as well. In fact, intuition is true knowledge. Insofar as knowledge becomes perfect, the variable possibility disappears. Since in God there is no variable will or arbitrariness, God's love is not narrow-

6. Nishida's note is "*Conf.*" Augustine (354–430) writes, "He does not will one thing then another thing; He does not will later something which He had not willed previously, nor does He cease to will something which previously he had willed. Such a will is mutable, and nothing mutable is eternal; but our God is eternal." Rex Warner, trans., *The Confessions of St. Augustine* (New York: The New American Library of World Literature, 1963), 294.

minded love in which God loves some and hates others, or by which some are caused to prosper and others to die away. The love of the God who is the foundation of reality as a whole must be equal and universal, and its self-development must be infinite love for us. There is no special divine love apart from the development of the myriad things in nature. Love is fundamentally the feeling that seeks unity. The demand for self-unity is self-love and the demand for the unity of self and others is altruism. God's unifying activity is none other than the unifying activity of all things, so as Eckhart says, God's altruism is God's self-love. Just as we love our own hands and feet, God loves all things. Eckhart also states that God's love for people is not an arbitrary action but something that must be done.

As discussed before, although God is personal we cannot view God as identical with our subjective spirit. God should rather be compared to the state of pure experience in which there is no separation of subject and object and no distinction between the self and other things. This state is the alpha and omega of our spirit and the true face of reality. Christ said that those pure in heart shall see God and that one who is like a little child shall enter heaven; indeed, in these cases our heart is closest to God.

As we have seen, pure experience does not indicate mere perceptual consciousness. There is a unity behind reflective consciousness as well. Reflective consciousness is established by that unity, and so it is a kind of pure experience, too. At the base of our consciousness there is always a unity of pure experience, and we cannot jump outside it (see part I). In this sense, God can be seen as one great intellectual intuition at the foundation of the universe, as the unifier of pure experience that envelops the universe. We can thus comprehend Augustine's statement that God intuits all things in the universe by means of unchanging intuition, and that God moves while still and is still while moving.[7] We can also glimpse the meaning of such expressions as Eckhart's "Godhead" (*Gottheit*)[8] and Boehme's "stillness without anything" (*Stille ohne Wesen*). A unity of consciousness transcends change and is unmoved; nevertheless, change arises from it. In other words, it is that which moves and does not move. The unity of consciousness cannot become the object of knowledge. It

7. Nishida's note is "Storz, *Die Philosophie des HL. Augustinus,* §20."

8. For Eckhart, the Godhead (*Gottheit*) is the impersonal ground of God's being and exists prior to any of God's personal characteristics.

transcends all categories and we cannot give it any fixed form—moreover, all things are established according to it. When seen from one angle, God's spirit is unknowable; when seen from another, it is closely connected with our spirit. At the base of this unity of consciousness we can make direct contact with the face of God. This is why Boehme said that heaven is everywhere: wherever one stands or goes is heaven, and it is through the deepest inner life that one arrives at God (*Morgenröte*).

Certain people might say that in my discussion God becomes identical with the essence of matter, or that even if God is regarded as spiritual, there is no distinction between God and reason or conscience, and that therefore God loses all living individual personality. Individuality can only arise from a variable free will. (In medieval philosophy, this is the gist of Scotus's disagreement with Thomas Aquinas.) We do not experience religious sentiment in response to such a God. Further, from my perspective, sin is not simply to break God's laws but to go against personality. Repentance is not mere moral repentance but sharp regret at having harmed one's parents and acted against a benefactor. Erskine of Linlathen[9] stated that religion and morality diverge according to whether personality is recognized behind conscience. But as Hegel and others have stated, true individuality does not exist apart from universality, and limited universality (*bestimmte Allgemeinheit*) becomes individuality. That which is universal is the spirit of that which is concrete. Individuality is not added to universality from without; rather, it has developed from universality. An accidental combination of various qualities without any internal unity cannot be called individuality. The freedom of the will, which is an element of individual personality, is a universal entity's self-determination. Just as the concept of a triangle can be differentiated into various triangles, to be aware of the possibility of the various determinations contained in a universal entity is to feel freedom. No individual awareness arises from a foundationless, absolutely free will. There is an expression, "In individuality there is no reason" (*ratio singularitatis frustra quaeritur*), but such individuality is identical to empty nothingness. My point is only that concrete individuality cannot be known through abstract concepts, although it can be clearly expressed by an artist's brush or a novelist's pen.

That God is the unity of the universe does not signify the unity of

9. Thomas Erskine of Linlathen (1788–1870) wrote on election (*The Doctrine of Election, and Its Connection with the General Tenor of Christianity*) and faith (*An Essay on Faith*, 1826).

an abstract concept, for God is a concrete unity or a living spirit like our individual selves. Just as our spirit is individual, God is individual, too. Reason and conscience may be part of God's unifying activity, but they are not God's living spirit itself. The existence of this sort of divine spirit is not a mere philosophical argument, but an actual fact of spiritual experience.

This spirit functions at the base of all of our consciousnesses. (Reason and conscience are its voices.) But when we are hindered by our small selves, we are unable to know it. The poet Tennyson had the following experience: quietly chanting his own name, from the depths of his own individual consciousness the individuality of his self dissolved and became an infinite reality. During this time his consciousness was anything but vague—rather, it was most clear and certain. He stated that death was a laughable impossibility at this time, and he felt that the death of the individual was actually true life. He also said that since his childhood, at times of lonely solitude, he had occasionally had this kind of experience.[10] J. A. Symonds[11] observed that as our normal consciousness becomes dim, the fundamental consciousness at its base becomes stronger until all that finally remains is one pure, absolute, abstract self. There is no limit to such experiences among religious mystics.[12] One might consider these phenomena unhealthy, but whether they are or not depends on whether they are rational. As stated before, if we assume that reality is spirit and that our spirit is simply a small part of it, then there is no reason to feel wonder at breaking beyond one's own small consciousness and realizing one great spirit. Perhaps it is our attachment to the sphere of our small consciousness that is most in error. Great people have spiritual experiences far deeper than those of average people.

10. Alfred Lord Tennyson (1809–1892) was an English Victorian poet whose poetry, to a large extent, addressed moral and social problems of his time.

11. J. A. Symonds (1840–1893) wrote on the Italian Renaissance, English drama, Greek poetry, and Walt Whitman.

12. Nishida's note is "James, *The Varieties of Religious Experience,* lect. XVI, XVII." These two lectures are grouped together under the title of "Mysticism."

CHAPTER 31

God and the World

Granting that facts of pure experience are the sole reality and that God is their unity, we can know God's characteristics and relation to the world from the characteristics of the unity of our pure experience or the unity of consciousness and from the relation of that unity to its content. First, we cannot see or hear our unity of consciousness, and it can in no way become an object of knowledge. Because all things come to exist in accordance with it, it totally transcends them. Although the mind conveys black when it encounters black, the mind is not black, and although it conveys white when it encounters white, it is not white. This characteristic unity of consciousness leads to the use of negation in Buddhism and in the so-called negative theology of thinkers in the medieval line of theology started by Dionysius the Areopagite.[1]

Such thinkers as Nicholas of Cusa stated that God transcends both being and non-being and that while God is being, God is non-being as well.[2] When we reflect deeply on the inner recesses of consciousness, we are struck by a lofty, mysterious feeling and discover profound meaning in Boehme's statements that God is "stillness without anything," bottomless (*Ungrund*), or "will without an object" (*Wille ohne Gegenstand*). In addition, God's eternality, omnipresence, omniscience, and omnipotence must all be interpreted from the character of this unity of consciousness. Because time and space are established by the unity of consciousness, God transcends time and space, is eternal and indestructible, and exists everywhere. And because everything arises from the unity of consciousness, God is omniscient and omnipotent; there is nothing God does not know and nothing God cannot do. In God, knowledge and capability are identical.

If this is so, then what is the relation between such an absolutely infinite God and this world? Non-being separate from being is not true non-being; a one apart from all things is not the true one; equality divorced from discrimination is not true equality. Just as there is no world without God, there is no God without the world. What I refer to here as the world of course does not indicate only this world. As Spinoza said, because God's attributes are infinite, God must envelop an infinite world. God's manifestation in the world accords with the essence of God, and it is never a contingent activity. It moreover is not that God at one time in the past created the world; as Hegel wrote, God is its eternal creator.[3] In short, the relation between God and the world is the relation between the unity of consciousness and its content. The content of consciousness is established by unity, and there is no unity apart from the content of consciousness—they are not two separate things, but rather the two sides of a single reality. In direct experience all phenomena of consciousness are one activity—however, by making this single activity

---

1. Dionysius the Areopagite, otherwise known as Pseudo-Dionysius, wrote a series of mystical treatises based on Neoplatonism. His exact identity and life dates are unknown.

2. Nicholas of Cusa sets forth the principle of *coincidentia oppositorum*, which maintains that in God's being the various polarities holding sway in the world of actuality converge, or more precisely, exist in unity prior to any division.

3. Hegel argues that the historical process is the continuing creation and revelation of *Geist* (spirit).

the object of knowledge and reflecting upon it, the content is analyzed and distinguished in a variety of ways. In the process of this development, the whole at first appears spontaneously as one activity and then, through contradictions and conflicts, its content is reflected upon and discriminated. Here, too, I recall the words of Boehme, who stated that the God prior to revelation—an objectless will—reflects on Godself, that is, makes Godself a mirror; therefore, subjectivity and objectivity are separated and God and the world develop.

Originally, the differentiation of reality and its unity are one, not two. What is called unity in one respect signifies differentiation in another. Taking a tree for example, a flower's perfect "flowerness" and a leaf's perfect "leafness" express the essence of the tree. The distinction between differentiation and unity derives from thought, not from immediate actuality. Just as Goethe said that nature has neither kernel nor shell but that all is simultaneously kernel and shell,[4] so in concrete true reality— in each fact of direct experience—are differentiation and unity one and the same activity. In a painting or melody, for instance, there is not one brush stroke or one note that does not directly express the spirit of the whole. For a painter or a musician, a single inspiration instantaneously comes forth and becomes an extremely varied landscape or an exquisite, complex melody. In this way, God is none other than the world and the world is none other than God. As Goethe wrote in his poem "Great is Diana of the Ephesians,"[5] silversmiths who earnestly made silver images of Diana without listening to Paul's teaching are in a certain sense closer to God than those who concern themselves with an abstract God in the brain. And, as Eckhart said, one sees the true God where even God has been lost.[6]

In this state of affairs, heaven and earth are merely one finger, and the myriad things and the self are of one body. Yet as stated before, due to the conflicts of the system of reality, and as the necessary process of its development, the system of reality comes to disintegrate; that is, reflection inevitably arises. By this means, that which was actual becomes conceptual, that which was concrete becomes abstract, and that which was one becomes many. At this point, God stands apart from the world

---

4. In the text Nishida includes the German: *"Natur hat weder Kern noch Schale, alles ist sie mit einen Male."*

5. The German title is *"Gross ist die Diana der Epheser."*

6. Eckhart is referring to the Godhead, where even the personal God cannot be found.

and the self stands apart from other things; each is relative to the other and one thing goes against another. In all likelihood, the account of how our ancestors ate the fruit of the tree of wisdom and were driven out of the Garden of Eden signifies this truth. The fall of humans occurred not only in the distant time of Adam and Eve but is taking place moment by moment in our minds. If we look at this in a different way, however, we see that disintegration or reflection is not a separate activity, for it is simply the development of the activity of differentiation that constitutes one facet of unity. At the back of disintegration and reflection lies the possibility of a more profound unity. Reflection is the route along which we attain a profound unity. (Shinran declares in the *Tannishō*, "If even a good person attains rebirth in the Pure Land, how much more so does an evil person.") For God to manifest God's most profound unity, God must first differentiate Godself. From a certain perspective, humans are directly God's self-realization. In terms of Christian legends, salvation through Christ exists precisely because of Adam's fall, and in all of this the infinite love of God becomes clear.

Considering the relation between the world and God in the above way, how should we explain individuality? If we assume that the countless things in the universe are manifestations of God and that only God is true reality, then must we think of our individuality as merely a false appearance which, like a bubble, has no significance whatsoever? I do not think that we have to view individuality in this way. Although there is probably no independent individuality separate from God, our individuality should not be regarded as a mere phantasm; rather, it is part of God's development, one of God's activities of differentiation. Just as all people are born with a mission given by God, individuality is an offshoot of divinity and each person's development completes God's development. In this sense, our individuality possesses an eternal life and constitutes an eternal development. (See Royce's discussion of the immortality of the soul.) The relation between God and our individual consciousness is the relation between the entirety of consciousness and one part of it. In all mental phenomena, each part stands in the unity of the whole, and at the same time each must be an independent consciousness. (In mental phenomena, each part is an end in itself.) In fact, that all things are the manifestation of a single, peerless God does not necessarily imply the negation of each person's self-aware independence. This situation is like an individual unity holding sway over one's consciousness from moment to moment while each momentary consciousness is an independent consciousness. Illingworth stated that one personality necessarily seeks another, and that in the other personality the self attains to the satisfaction of the personality as a whole; in other words, love is an indispensable characteristic of personality.[7] To acknowledge another personality is to acknowledge one's own, and the relationship in which people mutually acknowledge their personalities is love. In a certain regard, love is the union of both personalities—that is, in love, two personalities, while independent and respecting each other, join together and constitute one personality. Viewed this way, God can envelop all personalities and acknowledge their independence because God is infinite love.

The criticism of pantheistic ideas—such as the idea that all things are a manifestation of God—is voiced in conjunction with the problem of explaining the origin of evil. To my way of thinking, there is originally nothing absolutely evil; all things are fundamentally good, and reality, just as it is, is the good. Although religious figures forcefully preach the evils of the flesh, physical desire is not evil in an abstract sense; it only becomes evil when it hinders spiritual growth. Also, as asserted by ethicists relying on the theory of evolution, that which we now call sin was morality in a past era. Sin is the legacy of a past morality, which in the present age has become evil because it is now inappropriate. Fundamentally, then, things themselves contain nothing evil. Evil arises from the contradictions and conflicts of the system of reality. If someone asks about the origin of these conflicts, we can answer that they are based on the differentiating activity of reality and are a necessary condition for the development of reality. Again, reality develops through contradictions and conflicts. Although he constantly sought evil, Mephistopheles professed to be part of the power that constantly creates good. Indeed, evil is an essential element in the construction of the universe.

---

7. Nishida's note is "Illingworth, *Personality, Human and Divine.*" In this work Illingworth states, "We require to find in other persons an end in which our entire personality may rest. And this is the relationship of love. Its intensity may admit of degrees, but it is distinguished from all other affections or desires, by being the outcome of our whole personality. It is our very self, and not a department of us, that loves. And what we love in others is the personality or self, which makes them what they are. We love them for their own sake. And love may be described as the mutual desire of persons for each other as such; the mode in which the life of desire finds its climax, its adequate and final satisfaction." Illingworth, *Personality, Human and Divine: Being the Bampton Lectures for the Year 1894* (London: Macmillan, 1917), 38.

Because evil is not the activity of the unified advance of the universe, there is of course nothing in it that must be made into a goal. However, a tranquil, uneventful world with no sin and no dissatisfaction would be extremely mundane and shallow. Those who do not know sin cannot truly know the love of God, and those who have no dissatisfaction or anguish cannot comprehend the depths of spirituality. Sin, dissatisfaction, and anguish are necessary conditions for the spiritual advancement of humanity; a true person of religion does not see a divine contradiction in these experiences, but rather feels God's infinite grace. Such things as sin and anguish do not make the world incomplete; on the contrary, they make it rich and profound. If we were to rid the world of them, we would lose the way to spiritual growth and innumerable spiritual enterprises of great beauty would disappear from this world. If we assume the universe as a whole is established according to spiritual meaning, then there is no imperfection due to the presence of those things—on the contrary, we can know the reason for their necessity and indispensability. Sin is despicable, but there is nothing in the world as beautiful as a sin for which one has repented.

At this point I cannot help recalling a passage in Oscar Wilde's *De Profundis*.[8] Christ loves sinners as people who are closest to human perfection. It was not Christ's aim to transform an interesting thief into a boring honest person. With a method until then unknown in the world, Christ transformed sin and anguish into something beautiful and sacred. A sinner must repent, of course, and his or her repentance perfects the things done in the past. The Greeks believed that a person could not alter the past; they even had an expression to the effect that the gods were also unable to change the past. But Christ showed a way through which even the most ordinary sinner can do so. Wilde wrote that from Christ's perspective, when the prodigal son dropped to his knees and cried, he made the sins and anguish of his past into the most beautiful and sacred events of his life. Wilde himself was a man of sin, so he knew its essence well.

8. The Irish writer Oscar Wilde (1854–1900) wrote *De Profundis* (published posthumously in 1905) late in his career as a poet, dramatist, and novelist. The work consists of a long letter Wilde wrote to Lord Alfred Douglas while serving a two-year prison sentence in Reading Gaol on charges of sodomy. Benét, *RE*, 264.

CHAPTER 32

Knowledge and Love

*This chapter was not
written as a continuation
of this book, but I feel that
it is related to the basic
thoughts in the book, so
I append it here.*

People usually think that knowledge and love are entirely different mental activities. To me, however, they are fundamentally the same. This activity is the union of subject and object; it is the activity in which the self unites with things.

Why is knowledge the union of subject and object? We can know the true nature of something only when we thoroughly eliminate our own delusions and conjectures—that is, idiosyncratic subjective factors—and thereby unite with the true nature; in other words, this is possible only when we unite with pure objectivity. For example, the idea that the gray areas of a bright moon are a rabbit pounding rice into cakes, or that an earthquake is an immense catfish moving under the earth, is a subjective delusion: in such disciplines as astronomy and geology, we rid ourselves of all such subjective delusions and investigate things according to purely objective natural laws, and in this way we can arrive at the true nature of these phenomena. To the extent that we become objective, we can thoroughly understand the true nature of things. The history of the advance of learning over the past several thousand years traces the path by which human beings have discarded subjectivity and pursued objectivity.

And why is love the union of subject and object? To love something is to cast away the self and unite with that other. When self and other join with no gap between them, true feelings of love first arise. To love a flower is to unite with the flower, and to love the moon is to unite with the moon. The love between a parent and child comes forth only when the parent becomes the child and the child becomes the parent. Because the parent becomes the child, the parent feels each of the child's gains or losses as his or her own; and because the child becomes the parent, the child feels as his or her own each instance of joy or sadness on the part of the parent. The more we discard the self and become purely objective or selfless, the greater and deeper our love becomes. We advance from the love between parent and child or husband and wife to the love between friends, and from there to the love of humankind. The Buddha's love extended even to birds, beasts, grasses, and trees.

In this way, the knowledge and love are the same mental activity; to know a thing we must love it, and to love a thing we must know it. Because mathematicians cast off their selves and thereby come to love mathematical principles to the extent that they become one with the principles themselves, they can easily clarify the principles. By loving nature, uniting with it, and submerging their selves into it, artists can penetrate the truth of nature. From a certain angle, I love my friends because I know them. The more our circumstances are the same, the more our thoughts and tastes are the same; the deeper we understand each other, the richer our sympathy becomes.

But if we divide the two activities and think that love is the result of knowledge or knowledge is the result of love, then we have yet to realize the true nature of love and knowledge. To know is to love and to love is to know. When we are absorbed in something the self loves, for example, we are almost totally unconscious. We forget the self, and at this point an incomprehensible power beyond the self functions alone in all of its majesty; there is neither subject nor object, but only the true union of subject and object. Moreover, at this time knowledge in itself is love and love in itself is knowledge. When the mind is captivated by the wonder of mathematical principles and we become so immersed in them that we forget food and sleep, the self both knows mathematical principles and at the same time loves them. Likewise, when there is no distinction between self and other in response to another's joy and sadness and we directly feel what the other feels, laughing and crying together, then we both love the other and know the other. To love, therefore, is to intuit the other's feelings. When one saves a child who is about to fall into a pond, there is no room for the thought that the child is cute.

Love is usually considered a feeling that must be distinguished from pure knowledge. In actual mental phenomena, however, there is neither pure knowledge nor pure feeling. The distinction between the two is merely an abstract concept created by psychologists for academic convenience. Just as theoretical research must be maintained by a kind of feeling, so must love for another be based on a kind of intuition. Looking at the matter from my perspective, ordinary knowledge is of an impersonal object. Regardless of how personal an object of knowledge might be, ordinary knowledge emerges when the object is seen as impersonal. In contrast, love is knowledge of personal objects, and this knowledge occurs when the object is seen as personal, however impersonal it may be. The difference between love and ordinary knowledge thus lies not in the mental activity itself but in the type of object.

If we assume, like numerous scholars and philosophers have in the past, that the ultimate reality of the universe is personal, then love is the power by which we grasp ultimate reality. Love is the deepest knowledge of things. Analytical, inferential knowledge is a superficial knowledge, and it cannot grasp reality. We can reach reality only through love. Love is the culmination of knowledge.

I have discussed the relation between knowledge and love, and I will now consider this in connection with the facts of religion. Subjectivity is self-power and objectivity is other-power.[1] To know and love a thing is to discard self-power and embody the faithful heart that believes in other-power. If we assume that the work of one's life is not separate from

---

1. By these terms Nishida is referring to faith in one's own ability (self-power) to achieve awakening as opposed to faith in Amida's power (other-power) as the only way to achieve rebirth in the Pure Land and eventual awakening.

knowledge and love, then day in and day out we are functioning upon faith in other-power. Both learning and morality are the glory of Buddha, and religion is the culmination of knowledge and love. In distinct individual phenomena, learning and morality are bathed in the glorious light of other-power, and religion touches the absolute, infinite Buddha extending throughout the universe. The ultimate meaning of religion is conveyed in such expressions as, "My Father, if it be possible, let this cup pass from me; nevertheless, not as I will, but as thou wilt,"[2] and, "Is the reciting of the name of Amida Buddha really the cause of rebirth in the Pure Land, or is it a karmic cause of falling into the lowest hell? Of such matters I know nothing."[3] We can moreover know this absolute, infinite God or Buddha only by loving God or Buddha; in other words, to love God is to know God, to love Buddha is to know Buddha. Vedantic teachings in India, Neo-Platonism, and Gateway of the Holy Path-type of Buddhism[4] refer to knowing God, whereas Christianity and Pure Land Buddhism refer to loving and relying on God. Both views have their own distinctive features, but they are identical in essence. We cannot know God through analysis and inference. If we assume that the essence of reality is personal, then God is that which is most personal. We can know God only through love, through the intuition of faith. So it is that those who love and believe in God without knowing God are the ones who best know God.

2. Matthew 26:39.

3. *Tannishō*, section 2.

4. Gateway of the Holy Path Buddhism refers to the Zen, Tendai, Shingon, and Kegon sects, which emphasize one's own power. This expression contrasts with "Gateway to the Pure Land," which refers to Pure Land Buddhism with its emphasis on other-power.

Select Bibliography

TRANSLATIONS OF NISHIDA'S WORKS

Art and Morality. Translated by D. A. Dilworth and V. H. Viglielmo. Honolulu: University Press of Hawaii, 1973.

"An Explanation of Beauty." Translated by Steve Odin. *Monumenta Nipponica* 42 (1987): 211–217.

"The Form of Culture of the Classical Periods of East and West Seen from a Metaphysical Perspective." Translated by D. A. Dilworth. *Japanese Religions* 5, no.4 (1969): 26–50.

Fundamental Problems of Philosophy: The World of Action and the Dialectical World. Translated by D. A. Dilworth. Tokyo: Sophia University, 1970.

Intelligibility and the Philosophy of Nothingness. Translated by R. Schinzinger. Tokyo: Maruzen, 1958. Reprint. Westport, Conn.: Greenwood Press, 1973.

Intuition and Reflection in Self-Consciousness. Translated by V. H. Viglielmo, with Y. Takeuchi and J. S. O'Leary. Albany: State University of New York Press, 1987.

Last Writings: Nothingness and the Religious Worldview. Translated by D. A. Dilworth. Honolulu: University Press of Hawaii, 1987.

"Logic of Topos and the Religious World-View." Translated by M. Yusa. *The Eastern Buddhist* 19, no.2 (1986): 1–29, and 20, no.1 (1987): 81–119.

"On the Doubt in Our Heart." Translated by J. Shore and F. Nagasawa. *The Eastern Buddhist* 17, no.2 (1984): 7–11.

"The Problem of Japanese Culture" (excerpts). Translated by M. Abe and R. DeMartino. In *Sources of Japanese Tradition,* vol.2, edited by R. Tsunoda, W. T. deBary, and D. Keene, 350–365. New York: Columbia University Press, 1958.

A Study of Good. Translated by V. H. Viglielmo. Tokyo: Government Printing Bureau, 1960. (The first English-language translation of *An Inquiry into the Good.*)

"Towards a Philosophy of Religion with the Concept of Pre-Established Harmony as Guide." Translated by D. A. Dilworth. *The Eastern Buddhist* 3, no.1 (1970): 19–46.

Über das Gute. Translated with an introduction by Peter Pörtner. Frankfurt am Main: Insel, 1989.

SECONDARY SOURCES

Abe, M. "Nishida's Philosophy of 'Place.'" *International Philosophical Quarterly* 28, no.4 (1988): 355–371.

———. "Philosophy, Religion, and Aesthetics in Nishida and Whitehead." *The Eastern Buddhist* 20, no.2 (1987): 53–62.

Abe, M., and L. Brüll. "Kitaro Nishida Bibliography." *International Philosophical Quarterly* 28, no.4 (1988): 373–381.

Carter, R. E. *The Nothingness beyond God: An Introduction to the Philosophy of Nishida Kitaro.* New York: Paragon House, 1989.

Dilworth, D. A. "The Initial Formation of 'Pure Experience' in Nishida Kitarō and William James." *Monumenta Nipponica* 24, no.1–2 (1969): 93–111.

———. "Nishida Kitaro: Nothingness as the Negative Space of Experiential Immediacy." *International Philosophical Quarterly* 13 (1973): 463–484.

——. "Nishida's Early Pantheistic Voluntarism." *Philosophy East and West* 20, no.1 (1970): 35–49.

——. "The Range of Nishida's Early Religious Thought: Zen no Kenkyū." *Philosophy East and West* 19, no.4 (1969): 409–421.

Knauth, L. "Life Is Tragic—The Diary of Nishida Kitarō." *Monumenta Nipponica* 20, no.3–4 (1967): 335–338.

Takeuchi, Y. "Nishida Kitarō." In *Encyclopaedia Britannica,* 15th ed., vol.8, 723–725. Chicago: Encyclopaedia Britannica, 1988.

Viglielmo, V. H. "Nishida Kitarō." In *The Encyclopedia of Philosophy,* vol.5, edited by P. Edwards, 518–519. New York: Macmillan, 1972.

——. "Nishida Kitarō—The Early Years." In *Tradition and Modernization in Japanese Culture,* edited by D. Shively, 507–562. Princeton: Princeton University Press, 1971.

Index